Also by Deborah D.E.E.P. Mouton

Newsworthy: Poems

BLACK CHAMELEON

BLACK CHAMELEON

Memory, Womanhood, and Myth

DEBORAH D.E.E.P. MOUTON

HENRY HOLT AND COMPANY

NEW YORK

Henry Holt and Company
Publishers since 1866
120 Broadway
New York, New York 10271
www.henryholt.com

Some sections have appeared elsewhere, in slightly different form and with different titles:

"Black Woman to the World" first appeared in *The Texas Observer* (2019).

Material from "Dusting the Child from Our Bodies" originally appeared as "Double-Duck" in *Fjords Review* (2019).

"Drained" first appeared in *Queen Mob's Teahouse* (2019).

"Flying South" first appeared in *I AM STRENGTH,* edited by Alyssa Waugh (Blind Faith Books, 2018).

Lula, the Mighty Griot was a storybook opera adaptation with Houston Grand Opera (2021).

Library of Congress Cataloging-in-Publication Data is available

ISBN: 9781250827852

Our books may be purchased in bulk for promotional, educational, or business use. Please contact your local bookseller or the Macmillan Corporate and Premium Sales Department at (800) 221–7945, extension 5442, or by e-mail at MacmillanSpecialMarkets@macmillan.com.

First Edition 2023

Designed by Omar Chapa

Printed in the United States of America

1 3 5 7 9 10 8 6 4 2

For those who have had to shape-shift, code switch,
and camouflage just to survive, this one is for us.

Contents

I'm gonna tell you these stories.
Not all of them are real,
but that doesn't mean they aren't true.

To believe in me is first to know me fully. In the way one learns of a god's redemptive abilities at their first round with Death. This, so many refuse to do. Always take the power before I get a real hold on it. Black Woman. But I too am an ancestor. I too got a right to sit at Heaven's table and be served a plate. Deserve to inhabit my own jungle. I shape-shift behind the sun in midday. I learn from my mistakes. Give myself that permission. And I listen. Because even I have a mother. A griot in her own right, who tells me of the women who came before me. Of their all-seeing eyes. Their chameleon code switch. Their sticky tongues. Fastest on earth. Just like mine. I wonder how much of it, of me, I can tell you of before you are a new believer.

Let us see.

The Women Who Were Blind

My bloodline descended from the Women Who Were Blind. After making the sail from Africa, the ones who didn't sacrifice themselves to the sea, or escape in the Great Flight, adapted. Now settled on a plot between the Gulf and the dense trees, they wrestled to let go of the voyage. Having seen too much horror on the bottoms of those ships, they searched for a way to forget. In the late nights, when their captors weren't watching, they would sneak out into the tallest stalks and take turns pressing their thumbs into one another's eyes until it all went dark. It is easier to forget what you cannot see. It is harder to sell what is already damaged. So when the Women Who Were Blind bore girl children, they saved them the trouble. Called it a rite of passage. They would wait until they were old enough to walk. Then they took them out past the fields where the runaways hung like chandeliers in a grand forest ballroom. There, under the starlight, they showed their daughters all the sky's diamonds and then pressed until there was no more moon. The Women Who Were Blind called it mercy.

Over the next few nights, the Women Who Were Blind would hold their new daughters' hands and walk them through the forest, teaching them how to hear ahead and feel their feet anew. When they tripped, they would scoop them up and put them on their strong backs. The girls would weep. Then the Women Who Were Blind would sing them a hymn of the last drinking gourd they saw, until they were sound asleep.

Follow the drinking gourd

One woman, the one they called Fumbe, had a voice so enchanting, she could sing the galaxy smaller, make the ocean the sky's envy. She had received mercy early and now found herself with pregnancy put in her belly by the shadows and the stables. She would rub the sphere sprouting and sing it that drinking gourd song until the kicking quickened in her belly with hope. The other blind women around her would place their hands on her belly and wait for signs of joy. They would imagine her womb held the Messiah or Moses—some man to lead them far away from there. As her belly swelled, Fumbe tried not to entertain thoughts of another girl. She thought her hands too weak to do what would have to be done.

When the ninth month dawned, Fumbe waded out into

the Gulf until she was waist-high. The Women Who Were Blind surrounded her, gripping their feet into the silt.

They cried out for Yemaya to lessen the pain. When Yemaya heard them, she rushed to Fumbe. Her hands cradling Fumbe's belly. The ebb and flow whispering *Push*. Fumbe's water broke and she was one with the sea. Her child swimming forth with every thrust. The Women Who Were Blind braced her arms as she squatted and felt the newness fish from between her legs. Then the Women Who Were Blind scooped the child from the waters and held her high in the air, offering her up to the goddess. By now it was night and the songs of the cicada ushered them into praises for Yemaya's grace. Yemaya's golden-scaled tail caught the kiss of moonlight as she grasped the child and swam circles around Fumbe. The water danced and her chains chimed a welcome song in motion. She held the child for a moment before she placed it warm against Fumbe's chest. Then she offered a kiss and swam down into the sea, leaving a ripple of light behind her. At the first hold, Fumbe felt the braille of the child's face: a perfect nose, high cheeks, two eyes wide open to the moon. She glided her hand around its full belly and healthy legs until she felt nothing more. Then she held her daughter tight and wailed. She knew then her name must be Eshe, for all the life she would have to take was here in her arms.

Eshe bloomed early. Around six months, she said her first word as clear as rain: *water*. While strapped to her mother's chest in the fields, Eshe would pull at her mother's shirt until Fumbe would douse Eshe's head and arms from her canteen. The heat was unbearable and even Eshe had figured out the only thing that gave any reprieve. When the workday was over, and Fumbe had stumbled back to her shanty exhausted, Eshe would lay beside her and babble while playing with her mother's lips, nose, eyes—now patched over. Eshe was the light of Fumbe's day, in all her wonder and curiosity. Until the day she turned two.

Now that Eshe was old enough to own her steps, the Women Who Were Blind urged Fumbe that the time of mercy was upon her. So one evening, after the workday, the women lined the edge of the field as they had done so many times before. The air was thick and sticky. The Women Who Were Blind held their daughters' hands, with sight and with mercy. Those daughters still able to see were led out into the forest. Fumbe gripped tight to Eshe's hand and hesitantly pulled her along. The trees heightened, and the form of familiar fruit became more visible in the distance. Fumbe knelt before Eshe, fighting off the tears. She pointed up and told her of the stars and the Big Dipper. Then she promised Eshe the next part would keep them together forever. Eshe looked around and heard the screams of the other girls, but it was too late. Fumbe had hold of her head and began to tremble. The shrieks of the mercy echoed through the trees as Fumbe pressed harder and harder until there was no moon. Then she held Eshe tight against her chest. The two of them sat among the thicket, consumed by their own tears. Eshe cried herself to sleep, and Fumbe placed her on her back. When she tried to sing, she was muted by pain. Instead, she felt her way back to the group in silence.

The next night, Fumbe rubbed Eshe's head and promised the worst was over. Fumbe told Eshe that she had so many things to show her now. Eshe, patched about the eyes, stumbled as Fumbe pulled her out into a clearing a stone's throw away from the birthing place. Fumbe instructed her to listen. There was a way to hear direction just by how the wind blew through the trees. She told her to hear the rustle of the bushes; the small animals only hid west of the plantation. Fumbe ran her bare feet through the blades of grass until she found where the dirt bore its naked soil and the footprints of decades of women radiated warmth. She squeezed Eshe's hand, and just as quickly, Eshe's tiny palm squeezed back, before they both released and her child was free to discover her own air. The chill of her mother's absent guidance made her fearful at first. Eshe, in the way a foal stumbles before finding balance, toddled from tree to tree trying to get her bearings. Fumbe listened as branch breaks quickened with Eshe's growing confidence. The stumbling fall was usually soon to follow. But no cry ensued as Eshe felt for moss on the freedom side of the trees or as she used the willows' weeping branches to guide her through the canopy to the score of her own laughter. For a moment all was silent. Fumbe lost her daughter to the wind. The owl's hoo. Then

Eshe's distant mouthing of the word *water* just outside of her mother's reach. Yemaya's voice echoed as far as the sugar fields. Fumbe called Eshe back to her, but before she could grab hold of an arm, she heard Eshe's footsteps in the silt. Fumbe stumbled, heart pounding panic as she called out for Eshe's hand but instead heard her chant for water grow the distance between them. Fumbe swung wildly around until she began to run in the direction of Eshe's footsteps. She ran toward the faint splash. Just then, a rock found her about the ankle. Fumbe tumbled and hit her head hard on the earth.

When she came to, the Women Who Were Blind had collected Fumbe and brought her back to the shanty. She reached out for Eshe's hand but felt a hollow nothingness. The Women Who Were Blind said that Eshe found the water. That she must've gone out too far, just wanting to feel the rush of cool. They handed her the portion of Eshe's clothes they found snagged on the rocks. Eshe was gone. Fumbe mourned for three days before the anger set in.

On the morning of the fourth day, Sunday, she sought out someone to blame. As all were donning their cleanest rags, Fumbe was tying the last remnant of her daughter around her head as a declaration of war. As the church bell rang, she snuck out past the plantation grounds to the sea. She stood there on the coast, demanding that Yemaya show herself.

"Give me back my daughter!" she screamed. "How could you do this to me? What kind of god are you?"

Fumbe's fury woke the goddess from her slumber. Without warning, a large wave rose up and crashed into the earth, knocking Fumbe to her knees. Then the waters swirled into the image of Yemaya, her seven skirts dancing in the deep blue waters. Her cowry shells chiming in the wind.

"My child, why do you wake me with unjust indignation? And who are you to question my hand?" Yemaya pushed back like a steady wave.

"Give me my Eshe! How dare you take her from me!" Fumbe argued back.

"How dare I? How do you love what you refuse to see? Did I not hold your belly and lessen the pain? And what then did you do with this blessing? Take the stars from your own child's eyes? Turn yours from your own daughter's face? Did I not give her to you whole?" Yemaya approached with tears welling in her eyes.

"But you don't know what we have been forced to see," explained Fumbe.

Yemaya's anger now grew in place of her compassion. Her tears built into a wave that crashed into the shore, knocking Fumbe backward.

"Enough! Was I not there when the waters turned to blood? When the ships cut through me? Have I not felt your pain since the beginning? Am I not a mother too?" Yemaya scolded.

Fumbe cowered at the growing power of the goddess. "Then why take her and increase my suffering?"

Fumbe's anger broke. The tears began to stream down her face. She remembered Eshe's voice calling for her on their first visit to the woods, when her eyes were wide and the stars were still endless.

Yemaya calmed the sea and drew close. She held Fumbe's face in her hands. Fumbe had never been this close to a god before. Yemaya's eyes stared a hole straight through her, she could feel it. They must've held galaxies twisting and turning. Alternate endings. Second chances. And without another word, Yemaya saw it: the fear that had taken root in the back of Fumbe's mind. The one that risked everything to exist. The same fear that haunted the Middle Passage, that considered jumping from the side of the boat but never committed. And Yemaya knew, the way she always does, that Fumbe still had virtue left.

"Fumbe," she asked tenderly, "what will you do to have your child back?"

"Anything."

Then Yemaya commanded an electric eel from her hand. She offered Fumbe the path to get Eshe back. It would require a brave sacrifice. She must allow the eel to wrap around her neck in surrender. Death was certain in Fumbe's mind, but life without Eshe was unbearable. There was one last condition: Fumbe and her descendants must never again turn their sight from their children or their village. Fumbe was hesitant. She wasn't sure if she could face what lay behind her, but she knew no future would come from holding on to the past. She nodded her head and agreed.

With that, Yemaya commanded the eel to tangle itself around Fumbe's collar. It swam in figure eights until a searing pain burned through the back of her head. The sting leveled her to the ground. A bright light flashed before her eyes, and she was sure it was the end. Then she saw the sea stretched out before her. A large wave rolled in carrying the body of Eshe. It set her against the shore before calming. Fumbe saw Eshe clearly. Then she realized the taste of silt in her mouth. The pain struck her facedown, but somehow she could see Eshe rise from behind her. She felt her eyes, only to feel them still patched over. It was then that Yemaya's condition was clear. Two bulging new eyes had been burned into the nape of her neck. These never closed. Eshe came to her mother, and they embraced. Fumbe examined Eshe, only to find a second set of eyes already crafted in her neck. Every child born to that village, from that day on, was granted this gift. And so it is that every woman who dons this skin cannot run into the dark but must see the world in all its brilliant violence and horrifying beauty, lest their children lie at the bottom of the Gulf forever.

Spare the Rod

They say this story stays in all of us. The way trauma is passed through DNA. I can only assume so is survival. I don't come to this by casual assumption but more a reading of bones, or what is left after bones are gone.

I know little of those women outside their strength. Maybe even less of the ones on the other side of Genealogy's Brick Wall. I never met my great-grandmother Ma'Dea. But the way my mother talks of her, of all the women up the line of her blood, makes me believe in reincarnation, if only for a moment. Makes me see that the women before us left something in our genomes. A way to see out. They say that a memory changes its face every time you look at it. What is a memory anyhow, but a story you have heard rattle in you so many times that your mind calls it truth? My favorite truth happened long before I can remember. But my mother does.

The way she tells it:

It was during the swelter of an Alabama summer. Ma'Dea, who raised my mother as her own, held her by the wing. They fluttered into Kress, a five-and-dime store, something like a Woolworth's. This was back before integration. But the white folks didn't pay them no mind, long as they stayed in their own sky. The humidity itched up my momma's throat something awful and left her a wicked kind of parched. She slipped her hand from the nest of sweat building between hers and Ma'Dea's, flitted over a couple aisles in wander, and then beelined for the fountain marked *White*.

All the itch still climbing, she transformed into a plumage so vibrant, all the white folks stopped and stared. Tracked her with their eyes like they had pockets full of rocks and a hankering for stoning. To them, she was a leper, and there weren't enough angels stirring in that fountain to heal her from what they were planning.

Just then, Ma'Dea spotted her, like any momma would. Saw them sharpening their tongues on the rocks. Made her voice a trumpet to my momma's own rapture. Hollered, "Pat, wait!" And my momma froze, long enough for them to slide their hands back into their pockets. The corners of their mouths perked to approval. I guess it looked like the wild had learned the rules, like the Jim Crows could check their own chicks.

Just then, Ma'Dea saw them in all their happy and separate. Knew that, any moment, they could break their beaks for simply trying to scratch an itch. She saw my mother's bewilderment and decided to send a stone of her own flying back.

"Don't drink out of that one, it's dirty."

She pointed to the fountain marked *Colored*.

"The clean one is over here."

Momma says Great-Grandmother's mouth coulda killed her many a time. But how else could my great-grand teach my mother to traverse the past and the future? How else would I learn to be a tongue in two time zones?

She has always been a short thing, my mother. Five foot four in a house near full of six-footers. Skin of chocolate opal found near the Cahaba. Sang Marvin Gaye while teaching my brother and me how to build a sarcophagus for no-name Barbies. How to preserve the heart in a mason jar. How to liquify the brains and snatch them from the nose. We stomped bricks with our bare feet and baked them on our patio. We let Anansi and his pot of beans play in our eardrums before water fights and Skip It. She told us of Mahalia, Nikki-Rosa, Maya, and Nefertiti like they were the neighborhood women. Ones she grew up with. Ones we did too.

She rolled stories of sit-ins and water hoses in her mouth like revolution. Spat a sea of unfuckwithableness that turned our house into an island. Then she taught us to wade. To pray and wait for an answer. To take action in the quiet. *Faith without works is dead and don't nobody got time for that* when you are mastering chronoclasms.

She had a saying: "If you ever think the time will come that you are too big for me, I will break you at the knees and knock you back down to size."

She held all the smooth stones in a house of giants. She knew that soon, all of her children would be bigger than her, so she got her threats in early. Muttering something like:

If you are not careful, the goddess Enilder will turn you into a star. You will think of yourself more highly than us. Forget the days of cheese toast and sugar-dust sandwiches. Too celestial to ground your feet. You will think you are the all-knowing map. Move far, far away. You and your cul-de-sac wisdom. Will forget the joy of having nothing. Only return on the holy days. To kiss me with pity and hold to the outskirts of town. You will know someone took your cool, the way your mouth used to fold over slang. Occasionally slipping into your native tongue like an incantation of a former self. Apologizing before someone figures out whose you are. Seeks you out. And if I don't do it, the Lord will have to pull you from your own constellation.

Is that what you want?

She feared God as much as I feared her. But what is a healthy faith without a little reverent fear? Can you say you have spent time with a god if you have never been overpowered? It is the reason why we cloak. Why we only show so much of our glory every day. Why we only reveal our true selves in portions to those who prove themselves worthy. Why our children see us the most clearly. Why my mother felt the need to adapt. Leveraged her second eyes and some of her sanity for a job in espionage. She told us she used to work for an aeronautical tech company, but no evidence points to this being true. However, she showed us daily how she could stealth.

My older brother, Josh, was a trickster. Four years my senior, every moment spent spinning some web to catch me in. He was slim and lanky, like my father was when he spent his free time swimming, but branded with the kind of devilish smile that proved he was up to no good. He would trick me into believing that the hard-boiled eggs he put back in the fridge were turned solid by magic, only for me to try to splatter egg all over the freshly mopped floor. He would convince me that mudpies were made of chocolate, until I swallowed the first gritty bite. He would sneak in my room in the middle of the night and hide in my closets just to scare me. And somehow, by his weaving, I often found myself tangled on the wrong side of the almighty belt.

Maybe this was the time he convinced me that saying the words *damn* and *hell* were acceptable because they were in the Bible. I told my mom, "Damn, Mom, get the hell out of my room," and then instantly regretted it. My brother's jaw fell open in the guffaw of a fully executed trick, as she sniper-rifled the legs from underneath me with a single look.

I knew what whoopin' was coming for me. So I did what any rookie criminal would do—I ran.

I tried to find a place where the assassin couldn't find me. Lunged my body down the hallway toward the crawl space at the back of her walk-in closet. I knew she couldn't reach the deepest part of it. Watched her swat her hands before calmly standing, staring, and proclaiming, "I'm not gonna chase you." Then she wandered off to watch her stories. She hadn't given up. She was, after all, a spy. She had to be with us. But every 007 knows, some of the biggest threats hide in gentle words.

I bear crawled from the back of the closet, she nowhere in sight. I snuck down the hallway, trying to avoid every creaky land mine down the stairs. The TV began the *Days of Our Lives* theme, and she was locked in, but I couldn't let my guard down. She may have gone in the restroom. She might've stopped by the kitchen for a snack. She had proven one time before that she could make a Cap'n Crunch box feel like a whip against my backside, and my brother was always giving her a reason to crack it. MacGyver had nothing on the way she transformed a broom handle, book spines, and jellies into weapons of warfare.

From beneath the balcony, I watched her back settle into the beanbag upstairs. I typically had an hour for the rage to cool off as she watched another pair of twins come back from the dead to cheat on each other with their biological dad's long-lost stepson. I retreated to making amends, sure she would forget what I did with a sink void of dishes and a floor clear of Lego.

I cleaned for an hour before my mother came down and saw all the straightening up I had done. I held my breath, and she offered me a meal. She wouldn't poison me, would she? After watching *The Princess Bride* three thousand times, I knew the art of switching glasses. I waited until her back was turned and pretended to swap everything, including our napkins. She kissed me on the forehead and returned upstairs to her room to sing Andraé Crouch and scrub the tub. I heard the bass of gospel spread throughout the upstairs, and I was in the clear.

In a weird twist of kindness, my brother asked me to play paper cutouts with him. Occasionally his boredom would outweigh his need to torture me in the way brothers find entertaining. We cut the bodies off celebrities in magazines and assembled them into new beings. Centaurs. Minotaurs. Oprahtaurs. We pushed them across a giant poster board, crafting scenes and story lines. Before long, my smile returned and my guard dropped. We ate dinner as a family, on a large green tablecloth that inhabited the family-room floor. We watched TGIF, laughed together at that darn Urkel. When *Step by Step* finished, we all got ready for bed. First, room raids to clean up any remaining toys, then showers so our pores wouldn't be open in the morning. My mother always says that's how you get sick.

My brother's room was a powder keg of dirty dishes and

paper strips left over from the day's play, so he told me to shower first. I stripped down and turned on the hot water. There was a giant mirror that spanned an entire wall of the bathroom. When the steam was hot enough, it fogged over completely and became the canvas for finger graffiti. I wrote my name and drew a cat before I jumped into the shower to wash off the day. When I was done, I reached my hand around the partial wall to feel for my towel. I peeked out but couldn't quite reach it. I bent my arm farther around the wall, searching for the hook, when a warm talon grabbed my arm and yanked me from behind the curtain. My mother was crouching on the water tank of the toilet with a belt in hand. With one swift move, she pulled my entire writhing wet body up into the air and began to swat.

I. TOLD. YOU. I. WAS. N'T. GO. ING. TO. CHASE. YOU.

My body flailed and bent. I lost body parts and regrew them under the storm of my own tears. I screamed until there was no sound left to fuel my pantomimed cries, and my body collapsed at her feet, cold and wet and toppled over. Once she was done, she smiled. Kissed me on my forehead and said good night. Her calling card of love. The way Black mothers on plantations would beat the hell out of their children first to get grace from the master. Better it be done by someone who wants to see you alive.

Now before you call it abuse, you must understand what spoil lies in wait for undisciplined children. That a planet waits to cast stones and blame it on a wild child. My mother knew the great lengths Love demands. That Time sets different parameters. That this need for perseverance, that thing in our DNA, isn't always rational. No fight or flight is. It is a preservatory. It is selfish, the way that Black mothers are taught to silence. It says, if you are my child, you deserve the right of life. There is too much in you to lose. Even if it hurts me more than it hurts you, I know what sparing the rod might lead to. Even the gods have rules. And when someone broke them, it was a mother's job to redirect them.

My older sister learned that firsthand, long before I was born.

My three older, stair-step sisters, Denise, Monique, and T, all shared a father with me but spawned from their own shared mother. Their momma and my father called it quits years before. And despite the way their momma forced him to divorce his violin or wielded her words like a battering ram, their union yielded three beautiful girls who sprouted under the City of Angels' towering skyscrapers that cut through the sky like a legion of wings under the piercing sun. A halo of smog settled on the head of the brilliant metropolis of glass and Golden Globe, and the City held its own heavenly highway of stories.

My eldest sister, Denise, was born mute. Her umbilical cord danced too tightly around her throat in childbirth, but her mastery of ASL and her love of fried chicken and hidden candy under the foot of her bed made our twenty-one-year age gap seem trivial. She would con people who took pity on her stuttered step and chest-bound hand out of their money, only to sneak me some of it before turning her body into a trail of brown dust on the back of her boyfriend's motorcycle. The baby of their bunch, sixteen years ahead of me, was Monique. Smile like bottled lightning, slim like our father in all the tea-brown pictures of my parents frozen in the seventies. Always introduced me as half of her sister but loved running her hands through my wavy hair and the smell of new men. And then there was T right in the middle.

T was tall at every age. Eighteen years my senior, she was shapely and golden-boned. The only of my father's children to be blessed with his emerald eyes. Her long, pear-skinned legs seemed to go on forever. She was a child of the City. A brash tongue bent on surviving streets barred by blue-and-red feuds. She learned combat before compromise and was determined to make sure that my father's move to remarry and have more children didn't challenge the territory she had already marked out in his heart. After all, when your turf is threatened, the only answer is to fight for it. But she didn't know of my mother's power.

My mother was no stranger to issuing her own valiant blow. She did what the woman before her couldn't: she gave my father an heir. And T's momma hated my mother for it. The growing resentment of the new prince turned them into water and fish grease, popping off at every meeting. My sister was pulled between the two households, trying to draw new boundaries or at least hold on to the ground she already had. I don't know if it was the growing danger of being burned or an enemies-close thing, but the birth of the first boy in four pregnancies drew my sister closer to our father's nest. And somehow T was the only other child that ended up moving in with my mother and father, shortly after my brother was born, when they escaped the City for the refuge of the distant suburbs.

The Inland Empire was a different kind of desert palace. Rolling hills of dust and quiet streets surrounded what would become our suburban kingdom, as folks fled the City to build custom lives around us. Manufactured homes in the dry summer sold cheap in exchange for an hour-long commute back to the heart of the angels. The light pollution that made the angelic sky a scatterplot of planes landing at LAX and satellites dissipated under the rule of the night. Out in the Empire, you could still make out Orion's Belt. My father wanted to raise us somewhere we could still map out our way to safety. He stumbled upon our corner lot while ministering with a good friend. The ground was quiet, and the neighborhood was new. He knew this would be our fresh start. But T wasn't going to let fresh beginnings leave her behind. Her teenage allegiance to her own momma made her hell-bent on breaking mine.

She made sure to sneak out and ditch class often enough to keep my momma's instincts sharp, but, even at fifteen, she couldn't shake all her budding responsibility. That small sliver of adultness, that brooding compassion, she saved for our brother. When it came to him, she loved him like a leaf loves to shield the branch. She was his second mother, toting him on her hip at every chance. Rocking him to silly songs. If only she had found a way to obey the rules of my mother's new queendom.

My father often traveled for work, leaving my older brother and sister with my mother. One night, my mother left to take my father to the airport in the nearby canyon, where the roads narrowed and dipped, catching the fading sun behind the winding hills of the Empire. Both of them instructed her not to take my brother out of the house. My parents' rule was easy: "Nobody in, nobody out." It was nearing night, and the news stories proved that the city's danger wasn't as far away as once imagined. The streets between our desert oasis and T's stomping grounds had their own reputation for vomiting up the bodies of young girls in the wee hours. My mother had seen reports of brown feet toe-tagged in the industrial washes, highway shoulders, backwoods. If they would kill a young girl, what regard would they have for a child? My sister listened briefly, before the need for snacks or drinks, or the longing for the outside air, became a hook in her chest. She grabbed her jacket and packed up my brother. It would just be a quick walk to the store. They would grab a few things and be back before my mother knew it. They didn't plan on losing track of time.

Who knew T's friends would be hanging on the corner until the dollar movie started? It was just a coincidence that they were all heading to stash cheap snacks at the liquor store before they snuck into Richard Pryor's *Here and Now*. They would have snuck in the kid, but our brother's bedtime was approaching, and he was at the age of recalling every new word aloud at the most inopportune time. But that didn't mean they couldn't try to convince her. Time wandering down the storm drain. Evening slipping to night. I guess T didn't bet on how fast minutes could turn into hours. She also didn't bet on my mother dodging traffic like she was in a high-speed police chase.

My mother returned to find the house with the lights still on but no movement inside. She checked every room for bodies, calling their names. Then she began recon of the block. She went door to door to all of my sister's friends' homes. But all of them denied seeing her. My mother then tracked down my sister's boyfriend's house, but she wasn't there either. Knowing the way my mother worries, I'm sure the heaviness followed her from there. That it began playing movies in her mind. Altered news clips where my sister's green eyes and brown skin were all you could recognize. In her arms, a bloated chocolate ball of a child sat. She always jumps to the worst conclusions. With nowhere else to look, she drove all the way back home to wait for enough time to pass to call the police. But upon opening the door, she found my brother sitting in my sister's arms like they had been there all along. My mother laid into my sister.

"Where have you been?"

"Here."

"Oh, really? So you're just gonna sit there and lie to my face?"

"What are you talking about?"

"You think I don't know that you left?"

"I don't know what you—"

"You think you are just gonna take my baby and go wherever you please?"

Now, my mother says this is where my sister raised a hand to her. My sister says my mother became a deranged woman, loose about her mind, and attacked. The truth is a pendulum. My mother channeled all of her grandmother Ida Mae's power. I'm sure my sister summoned her own gods. Then the clash. My mother called my father's almighty belt to her, and it unbuckled itself from my father's waist and landed in her hand. My sister tried to duck and dive. She tried to outrun the belt that grew longer with each swing. First it knocked her clothes clean off her. Then it absorbed my mother's strength. With each returning syllable, bits of Black began flying off my sister. Each thunderous hit, another chunk of Black airborne. Until it finally happened. My mother had beaten all the Black off my sister.

The belt went limp at its conquest. My sister cowered on the floor, now a ball of red and bland flesh. My mother told her that the belt needed time to rest; then she would come back to turn her another hue. She closed the door behind her on her way out.

My sister wasn't one for waiting for danger to return. She grabbed some of our father's old clothes—a hoodie zipped up the front, oversize sunglasses—and headed out the back window like she had done so many times before. Jumping over the hedges, she slipped through the gate. She snuck down the block, ducking behind sheared bush and potted plant, until she found herself at the closest cross streets. She figured the council of friends might give her some advice on how to outrun my mother's anger. She found them tucked under the fluorescence of 87 octane, in the midst of parking-lot pimping. But as she approached, she noticed how their faces twisted. The closer she inched, the more concrete their shoulders and backs became.

"Hey, you guys, it's me, T."

She tried to push her way in, but the group wanted nothing to do with her. T overheard two of them talking: "Can somebody get this white lady outta here?"

Before now she hadn't looked down at what my mother had accomplished. The coal of her hands now a cooling ash. She stumbled from the group and found her reflection in the store window. All of her features were still there. But it was as if someone had siphoned all the amber right out of her. She pinched her arm to see if she was dreaming, but it just blushed red. She didn't know how to fix this, but thought maybe going back to the beginning was a start. She had to find a way back to her momma's house. Maybe she could reset her? The City has a way of reminding you who you are—and, I mean, after all, she did make her in the first place. But how would she get there? Her momma's house was over an hour away on the bus. It was getting late, and all the weirdos were starting to come out.

T thought that the store owner may have a phone she could use. Opening the glass door, the chime echoed through the store and the small, familiar brown man appeared. He had an accent thick like sugarcane. She didn't like him much. He had run her and her friends out of the store more than a time or two. He even had additional cameras installed to watch the neighborhood kids when they came in, after the last bell, to get Now and Laters and the Ninja Turtle popsicles with the bubblegum eyes. He swore they were going to fill their backpacks with Pabst beer and RC Cola when he wasn't looking. But this time, he was gentle. He even smiled, stood up straight. She sauntered through the aisles and picked up a pack of Lemon Cremes. But here, where accusation had met her so many times before, no one was paying attention. The in-store cameras were turned to the outside lot. There was no extra attendant unpacking items in succession with the aisles she shopped on. No one seemed to follow her. She even went as far as opening her purse before getting to the counter, and no one moved an inch. She searched the back wall for a telephone but found nothing but an overstock of generic tea and Kudos bars. A couple officers showed up just as she was pulling a bottle of water from the back fridge. She knew this drill well. Soon they would pull her to the side and ask her to empty her bag. She readied herself for the inquisition, but none ever came. Instead, the officers just tipped their hats and grinned. She watched them discuss something with the store owner. They fussed back and forth, pointing at the TV monitor that displayed the curb just outside the store. They quieted briefly as T paid for her items and left before things got any stranger.

Back out in the harsh lights, the officers rushed and headed for her friends. She watched as those who were too slow to scatter or too determined to reason were slammed against the sides of cars and shoved into the backs of cruisers. Most of her friends now lay facedown on the pavement, knees in their backs, backup arriving in haste. She watched the officers slam a few faces into the ground until blood spilled from more than one lip. A woman of a certain status drove up in the bustle. Her car sleek like the wildcat that protruded from its grille. She smelled like money and was clean like fresh bleach. She slid her body close to T's as she entered the store.

"Shame, isn't it."

"Yeah . . ."

"Women like us shouldn't have to worry about getting robbed on the way to get gas. I hope they lock them up for good."

I guess T looked like she would agree. And while she didn't, all words to argue back seemed to stick against the back of her throat. No matter how she tried to speak up, she was a prisoner to her own silence. The green in her eyes glazed over as the familiar bodies became more kin to the pavement. A fourth wall emerged, as she fixated on flashing lights and the nonchalance that settled in the crowd around her. The officers hurried her and the other bystanders along, saying there was "nothing to see here." But she couldn't stop staring, locked onto each body as they crumpled into the back of cop cars and disappeared under fleeting sirens.

By the time the cop cars had become ghosts on the horizon, the night had turned deep and unwelcoming. The warnings about "ditches and strangers with vans" echoing louder in the streets. T decided to beeline for the bus stop. It was the fastest and cheapest way back to her momma's door. She hopped on the 22 headed east. The bus driver made the men up front give up their seats for her. The bus was fairly empty; a few homeless men stammered through the door, paying their fee before bumbling to the back. One locked eyes with her, his glassy jet-black eyes gleamed from behind his dark skin. T grabbed her purse and clutched it tight. Why did she do that? This seemingly involuntary reaction. This route didn't stop in Fear as often as it did in Pity. She shook it off and looked out the window, watching for her stop. When she arrived at Wilmington and Alondra, she hopped off the bus and headed toward her mother's place. The neighborhood was grimier than ever before. Bodies wrapped in blankets in alleys. Late-night deals in plain sight. All of it now making her shoulders rise and her arms tighten. She crept through the street, avoiding eye contact. None with the late-night barbers who used to let her sweep up for payment under the table. Even less for the fishnet women who taught her how to dance when her momma was working the graveyard shift. The street that used to know her name like its own child now had harsh breath and an uneasy embrace.

With quick pace, she made it to the steps of her mother's home. The blue facade riddled with unruly cobwebs and a mailbox full of bills. She knocked hard. Her momma always sat in the back room and took her time when she wasn't expecting visitors. Before long, a shadow passed behind the iron screen and then disappeared. She knocked again.

"What do you want?"

"Momma, it's me."

"Me who?" Her momma peeked out from behind the door that crept open behind the dead-bolt chain. It opened wide enough to show her bulging eyes.

"It is me, T."

Her mother closed the door, as if to open it, but nothing ever came. T knocked again.

"Woman, what do you want?" T's momma yelled from behind the door.

"I want to come home."

The door now opened all the way, to the mouth of a Glock pointed clean at T's forehead.

"You ain't my child. This ain't your home. And don't nobody who look like you got a place here."

The door slammed hard. T staggered from the porch, mumbling her mother's words over and over in confusion, like a lost soul in a world that was willing to open its doors, but not willing to call her its own.

My mother said she didn't see T for a while after that. That it took her getting pregnant with my niece to bring her Black back. Not full tint, something more red-boned. It is something in the process of carrying new life that brings you to yourself. By then, my mother had moved on to birthing me and had given up trying to convince my sister of all the things she had to lose. Instead, she put her faith in me. The youngest of five, still trying to impress my siblings with thoughts of grandeur. Acts of disobedience. And my mother was more than equipped to handle my sass. I mean, I'm not bragging here, but I always had a quick-draw tongue.

Smartest mouth in the West from the age of five. Woulda held straw in my mouth, but I was scared of starting a fire. No time for tantrums when I could out-logic. *But doesn't lime Jell-O count as eating something green, Mom?* Shots fired. My mother would duck and dodge to the best of her ability, but no one was a match for the Clapback Kid. Though we would square off often. Her at one end of the hall with a belt in hand, me plotting how I would slide between her legs and take the roundabout through the wild stable where my brother was held. Bolt out of the back prairie to the open plains, where my valiant steed, Sarah, waited for me to jump on her furry back, pull her collar, and ride her into the sunset. My mother was not gonna chase me. But I knew it was 'cause I was too fast. Body and mind. A holster of fail-safes. *I'm just trying to do what Jesus would do, and didn't he flip the tables when he was mad?* Airtight. I kept a list of good behaviors at the ankle, and religion close to the chest. And when caught too close to desperation, I would pull out the big guns.

This one day felt like high noon. We stared each other down in the hallway, tingling fingers dancing over leather strip and excuses. Her heart pumping bigger than her chest. My confidence spreading a smirk like peanut butter across my face, smooth. I reached for an automatic to end it quickly. *If you touch me, I'm gonna call CPS on you.* Fire.

She dropped the belt. Calm-like saunters over to me. Her open hands soft. She slid her shoulder up to my chest and smiled. Took a big step back with an *okay* in hand. She pulled the phone book from her back pocket and flipped the yellow pages into a tornado that picked me up and held me just above eye level. She wrangled the phone from her front side holster and cleared her throat, graciously.

"If you feel I haven't been fair to you, feel free to call, but just know I don't raise no liars. If you call them, I will have to beat you."

Tumbleweed.

She put the phone in my hand and sauntered six paces before turning back. Her hand hovered over the belt buckle, itchy fingers returning, waiting for me to make a move.

Do you think she would do it?

What is dealing with the gods but a test? What am I if not handcrafted in her image? I got it honest, this tongue. This way to weave words into something more than a masterpiece of theater. This neck roll, this lip pop, this hand clap, this way to make a simple tale a dramatic feat. After all, for us, a lie is a story and a story is a lie. So I either am a liar or have mastered my mother's ability to concoct faith. Either way, my mother hated how I pushed the limits.

Upon unraveling the end of whatever tale I had fashioned, whether myth or legend, she would heave me into the bathroom, pull a bar of Safeguard from the cabinet below, and force me to scour my tongue with it. The milky white film plaquing across the roof and gums and cavities was supposed to teach me the dangers of using my powers for evil. Only, I don't know if I was a good learner.

One time, after a visit to the mulberry tree out back, she asked if I had ruined my dinner with raw berries. I told her no. When she asked why my hands, teeth, lips were blue-black and seedy, I spun a tale of a chief whose eyes were bigger than her stomach who tried to swallow the sky. Suspend disbelief. Maybe I was a chief in my own right.

Another time, I convinced my parents that I was not the door person at a party they didn't know I had attended, despite the fact that three snitches had given my name to the police as an accomplice. One of my best friends thought inviting half the school over while her mom and sister were at work would be seamless. We raided the pantry for food and moved all the furniture outside to create a larger dance floor. People poured in to Big Pun's "Still Not a Player." First underclassmen like us, then a sea of everyone. The two-story dwelling rocked at the studs until Chaos reared her head. Cloaked as a cute football player with a backpack full of porno VHS tapes and liquor, she hooked half the party in. When the other half were too busy grinding to music or sneaking into off-limits bedrooms, she needed another distraction. She called on the rain. All the furniture soaked to the frame. We panicked, pulling the drenched sofa and love seat back inside. Just in time for my friend's sister to arrive home early. Damn Chaos and her ruining. I bet no one washed her mouth out. I made my exit on foot. When I got home, my mother saw the fear in my eyes. I needed to get ahead of it. I told her that I was hanging out after school when people just started showing up. I wanted to leave, but I also wanted to be a good friend and keep her safe. Only half memories this time. By the time the sun had set, there were officers at my door asking if I knew where my friend was hiding. I didn't. But I wouldn't have told if I did.

Another time my mother told me not to roller-skate in the house. My sister left a pair of bumblebee skates in the closet. Back when she was natively Black and lived in my mother's house. Part of the plate had snapped on the right one. But my smaller feet could angle perfectly to keep it from bending. I was light and young then. The tile in the kitchen was roller-rink smooth. If I pushed off just right, I could bank my body and miss the oven, ricochet off the fridge, barrettes in full flight as I landed both hands on the double sink. Never mind the black skid marks all across the floor. I would wait until my parents ran errands, leaving my brother to watch me. Then I would triple double knot the long, frayed strands through the patinaed grommets and sing a web of songs as my dookie braids swirled around the kitchen.

I took this day as a perfect chance to practice skating on one foot, but I didn't anticipate my mother's early return. I guess she forgot her purse. I heard the keys jingle at the door just in time to make a mad dash for the hallway closet. I freed one of the skates, but the other, the broken one, wouldn't budge. In all my pulling, the strands knotted onto themselves and I couldn't get free. I heard the door pop open. Then my mother calling for me as her voice echoed through the kitchen, then upstairs to the den where she watched her stories. I yanked and yanked until I heard my mother's voice closing in on the closet. Her second eyes clueing her in. I could taste the slick of soap already. Here, pinned to the skates I wasn't even supposed to be wearing. I pulled my father's coat down from the hanger. I yanked the old luggage, anything I could find, and piled them on top of my foot as the door handle turned. Then I closed my eyes and begged for mercy.

"What are you doing in the closet?"

I bumbled out an answer. "I was just in my prayer closet with Jesus."

My mother held in the laugh that wanted to gurgle forth from her mouth. She pulled me out of the closet by my underarms, revealing the mangled boot entangled around my foot. Finally fed up with the mouth-bathing, she promised to tell my father when he got home. I have always been a daddy's girl, and my father was a Truth Conjurer. Had his own way to get the truth out of you. He wouldn't touch you, but he could make you feel simultaneously microscopic and immeasurable; a stain on the family name. I cringed for hours until his arrival. Time was more vicious than any lashing could be.

When my father finally entered my room, he sat on the foot of my bed and giggled. There was no need to tell him what he already knew. He looked at me square, like he saw my mother in me. Kissed my forehead and promised that there would be a Lie Catcher in my future. He said he would smell like fire and love me half as much as he does. And that would be more than enough.

And isn't Love someone we all want to believe in?

Can you touch my hair?
Can you pull a lion's mane
and expect it not to maim?

Between the Headache
and the Heartthrob

Love, like beauty, doesn't come easy. She has to be courted, tilled, washed, greased, yanked, and tied down every night. She doesn't get to build freely in the sun. She can't be knotted and kinked without scrutiny. This, a lesson better learned early.

My mother always wanted to cut off all her hair, but my father was against it. Rolled his eyes like, "What will I hold on to?" He wasn't ready to let go of the wavy Jerry curl that made activator run down the back of her plum summer dress when applied too heavy. Her mother had the same style. Both attempted to tame the thick, coarse hair that made them southern threats in their coastal corporate offices. Despite pictures of my cheerleading mother rocking a globe of joy over pom-poms in college, my father couldn't imagine her any other way. Years before me, she wanted a change—needed a fresh start after leaving her job and birthing the small umber boy that now adorned my father's arms. She wanted to find a new self in the mirror. Maybe my father read the story of Samson too many times, but he met every one of my mother's suggested styles in silent stonewall. So she settled on a compromise: he wouldn't cut his beard and she wouldn't cut her hair.

Until one day, my father had his own will in mind. Unsatisfied with the patchy nature of his face, he made the unilateral decision to go bare, without consulting my mother. Came home clean-shaven and young-faced. My mother took his actions as a breach of contract, one she had no hesitation making null and void.

On a women's retreat, she decided to do it. She was going to be a new woman. She sought out a friend with a barber background, and there, in the woods outside the City of Angels, where the redwoods reached their arms to God, she shed the weight of Black expectation until she was left with a glowing orb of boy-cut joy. It was sleek and polished; it was new and untreated. She rose, lighter, with a new sense of power pushing up into her glistening crown. And by the end of the retreat, her soul and her head felt closer to God.

When she arrived home, my father was there to greet her, my brother still in his arms. He smiled at the other women, offered hugs and charming conversation, but when his eyes fell on my mother, he went silent. Where all that was needed was a single word of affirmation, my mother watched his green eyes brown in anger. He withdrew from her. My justified mother softened. The crown that once pulsed to glistening seemed less lustrous in the cold punishment of my father's silence. And when my mother finally mustered up the resolve to seek out an explanation, she found that he was furious that she moved out of his timing. He forgot that our bloodline often does. I am not sure if his disapproval had anything to do with it, but my mother's hair only grew after that. From a flattop through the late nineties to locs dangling at her tailbone by the time I was old enough to leave their home.

I guess she figured being heard came second to being held. The things we sacrifice on the altar of Love. We all want it smooth like the pictures. Like the fairy tales of blond ladders and tower deliverance. Like silk strands blowing in the wind. The ones that have never broken a comb, or woken up coiled with an attitude.

I remember wanting to be that kind of loveable. Rummaging through pictures of Hathor and Oshun, seeing nothing like that in the mirror. Trying everything to tame myself into something more dark and worthy. I remember praying for my mother to make me something people could devote themselves to:

Momma, make me a girl for Picture Day. Pull the blue dress from the closet back. The one with the happy face flat on the chest. Test the metal straightening teeth till the paper towel doesn't brown. Burn my head beautiful. Bite me at the root and yank the kink halfway down my back. Make me look like the girls in *Teen Vogue*. It's the seventh grade. My legs are lanky and my breasts are coming soon. It's the Lord's Day. So make it straight and narrow. Slick back my edges. Slip the prongs against my tender scalp. Wrangle every baby hair close enough to wince. I want to be sleek, gleaming in the sun. I want to not sleep between the headache and the heartthrob. Where the pretty lives. Then the boys can see that I'm not one of them. That I am a lady. One it is okay to love.

Holy utterance. My mother laid me across the counter, pushed my head into the large metal sink. She yanked and pulled and greased. She blew a thousand winds until I was a head full of frizz. Then she heated the comb white-hot. Blew cool enough just to sizzle. An eternity later, she had done it. Like a trick stirred in a cauldron of Blue Magic. She had pressed the steel wool into fine twine. I was unrecognizable in the best way.

Before I left the house, she knighted me with a wooden safari necklace strung around my neck. Hand-carved spotted giraffes and mahogany elephants. Draped a zebra hide around my body. Told me how Nefertiti I was becoming.

When I arrived at school, I gazelled my long legs across the quad. Each lazy Susan head twisting to gawk and whisper. I was firsthand-royalty stunning. The kind that made my guy friends feel uncomfortable talking about the girls they kissed. And the girls . . . the ones who found all pleasure in joking about how I was more man than model, were hypnotized before my very eyes. The palest girls' eyes widening in awe as the other Black girls' jokes about my unkempt kink turned into nods and curtsies of approval coupled with every other minute spent asking if I *finally* got a relaxer or a compliment about how I must've absorbed the moonlight overnight. My knee-bending mane billowing behind me in a train of golden threads, crossing the quad, catching all the sunlight so violently it must've cracked the sidewalk. Wrung the trees dry. Moved the skies to such heavy tears. Voodoo of rain. And faster than my legs could retreat, torrential, my crown recoiled to a shrunken head. And all of them shed their kindness. Turned all den of seething cobra midstrike.

Our teacher attempted to snake charm them back into civility in the gymnasium, but the laughter was already too venomous. I stood before the magic camera, too afraid to look up. To show everyone my dark, my unfair. The camera shattered at the first flash. And I was left with no idea how to reverse engineer all the ways I had failed to be gorgeous.

My mother spied me sprinting toward the car at the last bell, trying to flatten the beast with my hands. She is nothing less than devout. Before I could crumble, she smiled and promised to help. She, who boasted a perfectly groomed flattop, said I must find a way beyond her way. She said, unlike her, I am blessed with good hair, just too much of it. In the next breath, we were spying down the long aisles of the beauty supply. The woman with the hawk eyes watching from the cash register as I caught my ivy hair climbing, more feral with every passing mirror. I read the bottles. The endless choices to curl, to straighten, to hold the frizz; so many bottles of control. I wondered what it would take to train me. Momma said the three hours every week could be better spent. Tired of the sore arms and the breaks halfway through. Then there was the shrieking. She said I must be trying to wake Death; she thinks Death sleeps. Then there is the Holy Ghost flinching, the crying out her name. I couldn't help how the holy hurt. I needed to find a bottle right with my name. Something just for me.

My mother said not to lye. So I found a box that had a little girl's face. Smiling pretty and brown. The waves cascading down like she was part waterfall. I wanted to be that kind of aquatic. I showed my mom. She nodded. The hawk-eyed woman hoped this decision would make us leave faster. She was tired of missing her stories on the box television. My mother paid her, and the spell was wrapped in a black plastic bag.

When we returned home, I was eager to crack the seal. My mother didn't hesitate to start the ritual. She pulled the ivy from the scrunchie, and I tried not to shriek. She sat me on the counter and leaned my head back, deep into the metal sink. I felt the water rush and the ivy become docile, if only for a moment. Then I was one step from being the ocean herself.

A slather of Vaseline around the edges. A dollop of magic. Cream smoothed to the skull. And then the not-scratching. Scratching brings torment. A haunting, they say. This is why every girl learns of Miss Mary Mack early. Our mothers' way of warding off the itch. I sat until I smelled the spell working. Then the tingle that said it was time to see how my people may have been part sea. My mother dipped my head back into the sink and pulled the coil faucet head that extended the spray. The rush of cool washed away any embers of magic.

My mother told me to run, go look at myself, how I had changed. I found a looking glass, and the light rippled down my back. I ran my fingers through my hair, or rather, my hair ran through my fingers. Clump after clump. I offered a familiar scream, and my mother came running. We frantically tried to piece me back together, but the strands ran out too fast to catch. Magic revoked as fast as a fear takes hope. No more beautiful than a stagnant lake; a stench that wants to be an aroma; a false god's trick just wanting to be believed.

I spent the next six months mourning. Is it weird to say that I too know how to mourn myself? That I have limitations? That I need saving? Or at least time to grow back into who I was. A tail snatched off doesn't regenerate in an instant. Love takes her time, sometimes. Especially when all you want to be is yourself.

The best spies know that the key to blending in is maintaining your cover. My mother included. She tried to play the game for the first year after my father accepted his calling at Calvary Southern Baptist Church. It was a tan-colored worship space too big for itself and too bland to stand out among the roaring dust storms that plagued the Empire's falls. My father agreed to support their congregation as interim pastor while they searched high and low for someone to maintain their white-gloved, good-ole-boy tendencies they snuck west years ago. My mother was the furthest thing from the demure Southern belles they had become used to.

The Southern Baptist had a flare, a way of performing. They were not quite at the COGIC level of bold printed suit linings and magenta crocodiles that I saw when I left to attend school near the City of Motors. Every preacher there looked like he escaped from a Motown revival to go solo in his own pulpit. Head with three-quarter part and tapered fade, dabbing sweat from his brow as the choir became his background dancers, robed in crushed velvet even in the summer months. First Lady by his side in a fur coat and a matching hat. Guess when your people migrate that far north, every day is a celebration. But the Southern Baptists did have one hundred women in white expectations.

My mother tried to find her own balance. She stuck to calf-length skirts and A-line dresses, the modest sheen of a flat-ironed head. She stayed quiet by his side; tried everything to be a good pastor's wife, minus the hats. She tried to maintain the press and curl that made her respectable and approachable to parishioners. Much of it was done with a quiet smile, as she held her space tied to my father's hip at community events. But blending is a temporary solution, camouflage is meant for fast fleeing.

Near their first anniversary of being in ministry, my mother looked in the mirror and had trouble recognizing herself. Maybe it was the approaching empty nest or the distance between her Black and all the various shades she had become to fit in. She knew something had to shake. So she took hair between the tips of her fingers and started to twist. At first a discovery of sorts. She had been bridging the gaps between her identities for so long that nothing was permanent. But here, in the long-glassed mirror, her hair offered its own resolve. And as she turned each soft kink upon itself, a click. The hair locked. It offered the weight of a dead bolt, but not in the way we keep things out, rather the way we keep safety in.

She turned another clump of her black cotton until it clicked into place, then another. When her hands finally stopped moving, her head was a crop of bundled nubs, lying neatly against her glistening scalp. She had not defied my father's request or bowed to the congregation's standards, but she was finding a way to make the limitations of this world her own.

When the time to celebrate came, she planned out the big unveiling. My father instructed the attendees to come casual, an unheard twist of fate. My mother entered the sanctuary for the grand reveal, wearing a golden-mustard kaftan draped over kitten-heeled Jesus sandals. Not quite the suit or shift dress they wanted. But not hiding anymore. Her dreads sat no longer than an infant's waving fingers. My father's dashiki-wrapped body joined hers hand in hand. They were a united front, a king and queen floating down the aisles between every pew to the whispers that followed.

"Why didn't she wait until after *this* for all of *that*?"

"Did she forget to do her hair?"

"Why did he let her do that to her head?"

But my mother paid them no mind. For what is good without a hater's evil to balance it? A spy without a criminal organization to infiltrate? People and all the ways they try to cut down. But Love has been reduced to the ground so many ways before. She takes pleasure in the regrowth. And despite the ugly phase, the awkward trial of growing into yourself, my mother found something and someone to hold on to. A way to reclaim herself all Black, all woman, and loved.

Maybe there is a place I can go that will teach me how to master that. How to be held and be heard. A classroom of sorts. Where, there, stained into the walls, I can teach myself how to turn silence into strength.

* * *

I find myself in Space City. I am south, just outside the inner ring that makes the City look like a bull's-eye to the naked eye above. Maybe that's what NASA uses to pull the space-crafts back home. I have been in orbit for a few years now. I float across the sprawling southwest galaxy in search of an anchor. I am old enough to be considered an adult, but young enough not to be required to have all the answers. It's the second-to-last day before the students return to our parochial high school. My name is still freshly minted on my classroom door from a year earlier, but before we can wel-come a single young mind back into the building, the staff and faculty gather in the multipurpose room to discuss the state of the school, upcoming policy changes, and student survey results. The PTA generously provides donuts, fruit, breakfast tacos, juice, coffee, and conchas from the panadería down the street, in a glorious array of deliciousness, putting everyone in a much better mood. I stand near the back of the room with my friend Lupe and some of the Black faculty. The training will be long, and the grated metal chairs weren't made for a woman of my girth. Standing also affords me the advantage of seeing the entire room. People have a tendency to show you their true colors in the smallest tics and facial twitches.

We arrive at the part of the day when we must discuss the bane of every teachers' existence: the dress code. The distributor has changed, and the girls won't be able to roll their knee-length gray garbs into tantalizing miniskirts with knee-high socks anymore. There has been a change from senior T-shirts to polos. Athletic shoes are not allowed. The eyes roll. The hands begin to doodle boxes around boxes. The bodies shift in their seats to complain that it is enough. There is a debate on whether black leather Jordans count as athletic shoes. The dean wants students to be clean-shaven, "no colored hair" he says. The sighs. The phones unlock. The occasional hands wring or raise.

There is one. A stubby tan hand, just dark enough to claim color, raising high over thick oiled-back black hair. I stand behind it but recognize it immediately. It's the same hand that rumors say reached under a female student's skirt to "pull it down" in the middle of class. It's the same hand that moves to make copies in the staff lounge as he explains that his Spanish descent makes him more tolerable and refined than the immigrant students we teach. Before I can brace myself, the question assaults: "So what are we gonna do about this nappy hair and dreadlocks?"

My legs jockey back and forth for a way out. I bite my lips, and I can't hear anything, and then I stop and look around. All of the white people have seen us. Danyell, Crystal, Angela, and me, all at the back of the room with our untamed hair and twisted crowns. I run my hand through the puff of my ponytail as Crystal's eyes widen. Her hand becomes a rocket launching through the tense sky.

"Do you mean natural? The way God naturally let my hair grow out of my head?"

The asking hand is now resting on its lap. Its back hasn't turned to acknowledge the growing uproar around it. It is solid, secure. The voices with no stake begin to chime in about how they feel "uncomfortable" with the subject. The dean says we just need to maintain "professional standards." And we all read between the bars. The gate has closed; once again we are on the other side. The conversation finds a way to be tabled until tensions settle, and we are dismissed for lunch. Allies for each camp separating to cut eyes and teeth on one another's words.

I survey the room. Every Black body holds an untreated mane and a bit in their mouth; one we are supposed to eat around and still get full. I swallow a week of sunrises trying to burn the voices in the pit of my stomach. Trying to quench the hunger in me to be accepted.

But I guess, if learning came by simple means, we all would be teachers. A proverb among the gods says that those who instruct have the harshest judgment. They sacrifice the joys of life for a life of lessons. If only sight didn't burden me with this yoke of soothsaying. Of knowing what lengths we must go through to craft a moral for the young. But learning to love, down to the root, takes digging. Takes pruning and big chops and sacrifice. Takes being hungry enough to erase everything you have gained for something you could lose. What a world this education is. In every time zone, no matter how we weave it, there is always someone waiting to make us question the very thing we know to be right.

Somedays it's hard not to look at myself and wonder what they think of me. Am I less saintly now? Should I straighten my hair to be more divine? My heart cringes at the smell of ceramic, lye or no lies. I have wished myself a thousand heads to logic the answer. I have even tried to replace the nagging silence with the roaring worship of my students' laughter.

As the other teachers creep at a zombie's speed and attempt to finish making copies of neon bathroom passes and syllabi before the bell, I visit myself in every hall door. Making sure there is no room for questions. No strands out of place. No way to make my most indigenous parts seem foreign. I turn myself into the color of a smile. I welcome the new school year like I have learned the true meaning of mercy. I pass Steve and ask him how he is doing. He responds, "I am either pumped or about to shit a brick." I laugh.

I head into the morning assembly trepidatiously hopeful. We line the sides of the halls with marigold and yellow inflatable bam bam sticks to welcome the students back to school. The tan hand, and one of his cosigners, stands across from me, apathetically staring at the doors. But then they pour in.

My children, in the way we graft the young onto our hearts. Their shirts neatly pressed under their navy cardigans and blazers. Some smile, some cringe, all of the freshmen are overwhelmed by the reception. Some have grown their hair out, others have shaved it down to a nice fade. Some call me "mom" and hug me. Others whisper hello under the beating pulse: the crescendoing clave of applause.

One student gallops through in grandiose fashion, always the class clown. His body is long and streamlined. His arms are brown and jutting in every direction *hello* can run. Everyone remembers him being much more untamed last year. The kid who couldn't sit an entire class without examining the furball of his own afro now has a head of the crop god's glory. A field of the finest rows of corn. Edges laid back as the summer. Maybe this year he will be worthy.

We head into the assembly and pray. We cross our hearts with our hands and pray. We ask to be made men and women for others. Learn to be open. Love unconditionally. We pray. We pray. We pray. In the name of the Father, Son, and the Holy Spirit.

The teachers are dismissed, and I head to pick up my remaining copies from the workroom. But before I can enter, Danyell sees me and says, Did you see the harvest? That field of maize planted with such grace? His mother's two-hundred-dollar sacrifice? Did you see how his head was a plantation's glowing bounty? Did you know that *they* asked him to scythe?

"Who is 'they'?"

She says the dean mentioned it was *unprofessional* and told him it had to be ripped up by the end of the week. And here we are again, waiting for someone to approve us.

Watching our children endure being planted in a field that only yields their kind of harvest.

But this is not the archaic timeline where I give in. In this one, I am the tinge of wildfire. I pull a chair up to the dean's desk and park it. Ask to see his Clothing Commandments in stone. He refuses at first, but then reads them aloud, as if the proclamation will come down on its own might. He slows when he realizes that his bias has no formal language. "No hair past the shoulders" doesn't apply when it is braided taut to the scalp. He backpedals. I push back. He explains that something must be done with them. I hear *them* like a tree snapping. He sees I am two steps from jumping over his desk, the way a spark does a five-lane highway, and he backs down. I quell. Stand and leave a trail of ash as a reminder.

I smolder in the hallway, until I see that the head of bounty has opted for hallways over instructional time. I call his name, afar off. And he comes quickly. I tell him how his mane is the epitome of sacred. He repeats *their* words as if they have weight. So I teach him. There is no room for you to cower away from yourself here. If they tell you how to shrink, show them to my blaze. He nods and smiles.

There is nothing new under the thumb. Though to say one can love all of oneself is its own kind of fantasy. There is not always this much color available. I would be remiss if I spoke of this stand like it existed in every reality. No, sometimes the worlds don't converge ideally. Sometimes the story gets too powerful and makes us a prisoner of war.

Sometimes we have to fight back. I have taught this to my daughter already. How to pick and pat holy, without repent. What dangerous thoughts I have put into her head.

All things kink in the night. My daughter has learned that no satin cap or do-rag can undo this truth. So on Sunday mornings, we rise early. I baptize her head over the sink, like my momma did me. Watch as her eyes close and she mumbles a prayer that each tangle would be kind in its unraveling. I sit her between my legs, and the righteousness comes in. Dip my hand into the dew of shea and moisten the dandelion tufts of hair that open with the light. We pray. We sever the fairy knots from their webbed descension. She tries not to cry in the face of God as I pull each bundle into its section. I remind her what a blessing it is to have all this burden. I run the comb from end to scalp, shaping it all into a pappus of brown. A trinity in hours that springs forth in wave and 4b pattern offered to the wind of the day.

Her favorite mornings are when we float as far as the donut shop. The one that orbits under the yellow awning and is run by the nice brown family that gives us extra donut holes. We squeeze between cars in the full parking lot and join the line that stretches out of the building and halfway down the sidewalk. This day, when we finally step foot on the large tile squares that say we have arrived, she quickly runs to hover in front of the glass display, fawning over the polished sweet rings. A woman tumbles behind in line. She watches as my daughter twirls and bounces with the current, pointing at every sprinkle and design with intrigue and wonder.

She takes her hand, in all its invisible grime and wonder, from her pocket. Her fingers spread, lurching her dusty grip toward the glow. My daughter's eyes are too busy dancing from kolache to cinnamon twist to notice the full, strange palm sliding against her hair. The way a child yanks a flower from the earth and blows. All her seeds springing out the door. Orb caving into itself.

My daughter flinches, but the villain's hand is persistent. She looks to me, and I signal, in the way that we often talk without words, to do what we have practiced. She closes her eyes. Then her hair hardens and morphs. It opens its jaws wide enough to gulp. Chomps down on the woman's wrist. The glass shield is now the color of strawberry jelly. The mouth rolls the crunching arm around a bit before chucking the severed limb out in repulsion. The woman thrashes about on the floor, screaming into a stump as if she can reattach herself in yell. My daughter, unbothered, takes to my hip.

I comfort the fierce being. Stroke its back until it is fast asleep. I buy my daughter one of the pink confections with the rainbow sprinkles. Her mouth is a speckled smile as we step past the incoming paramedics. Over the contagion of poppies billowing on the floor. I tell her to keep this power to herself. One she only needs to share with God, her mother, lovers who prove themselves worthy, or anyone who tries to get too close. And she agrees.

The world has nothing to lose on us, especially when we don't believe we can win. And I wish I could tell you that age has given me Athena's confidence. That immortality has proven that "beauty lies within." But what I can assure you is that I am no longer a slave to any head besides my own. And maybe it's time I weave that into a story.

The Beholder's Bewitched

The beauty shop is its own temple. Large casted thrones with bubble crowns that shower heat. Libations of melted bergamot and steel baths of holy water in sacrament. A sew-in is a sermon, a lace front its own lyric. My aunt Angel, in the way that Black girls play Slide with sticky hands and call everyone who sticks family, came to worship every month. She would stand before the Crop Gods seeking their blessing. Sometimes four hours, sometimes sixteen. Angel welcomed the blessing of Brazilian Human Virgin Natural. Boasting in hair flicks of long lengths and bobs switched at a moment's notice or lasting eons. The heavenly glow of prestretched and Remy in sheen masked any of her kitchen's sins. The coil and kink was tamed here. Even if only restrained in cornrows.

Her edges, on the other hand, seemed to have a mind of their own. Angel's religiosity was the only way to keep the sin of her edges under wraps. They rebelled, constantly pushing up and out to protest the way the gods controlled them. Angel hated the young hairs that refused to learn any discipline. No matter how much black gel she slicked on or how many toothbrushes guided them back to her righteous forehead, they were unreasonable. So she would rise early on the fourth Saturday of every month and bring offerings of coin to the Crop Gods' feet.

Angel's edges despised the gods' desire to know everything, to hold it all down and in its place. They would spend weeks plotting and planning their escape in new growth, only to be roped down. Micro, box, crocheted, Marley-twisted arms and legs, warping them into another sentence at Angel's request. Then she would entrap them in a scarf, Fumbe's armor, to ensure ultimate dominance. They would grumble, facedown on the scalp, wishing the gods would repent.

The Crop Gods were burdened with too many other requests to be bothered with the lowly edges. They ruled with an iron comb. Some people came to worship it emerging hot from the holy embers; others begged to have gold threaded to the bone. They, draped in smocks of silk, flaunted cans of fairy dust and tongues of rhodium, with the patience only omniscience could grant. They were no friend of wild curls or rogue strands that sought their own agenda. So when Angel would spot the newness trying to frizz its way out, she would rush to the temple, pushing and shoving among the eternal line until the gods shined their grace upon her.

It wasn't until the fourth Friday after the crescent moon that Angel found too much freedom in the night music. The gyration of her body to the beat gave even more liberation to the growing grumble of angry edges. The humidity loosening them to coil. They gained strength. The more wild they became, the more free Angel felt, swinging her head and body-rolling herself into the dusk. By the end of the night, Angel's edges only needed an opportunity. Her fatigued forgetfulness to tie them down, the perfect moment.

Angel rose early, hungover from the freedom, on the day set aside for worship. She swung her feet to the side of the bed, dizzy from the previous night's wild. She yawned and ran her fingers across her face only to feel more forehead than usual. The light flushed out of her as she rushed to the mirror. Her cheeks filled with burning coal as she looked in the glass to find her edges gone.

The shrill tremble shook her room down to the studs. She began tossing clothes on the floor in search of the missing edges. She searched in the cabinet, pulled clumps from the drain, even dumped out her entire makeup bag, but the edges had been snatched. Her eyes began to feel like a rising river.

"What will I do without my edges?" Angel mumbled to herself as she looked into the growing Magic 8-Ball of her forehead.

"The gods must know what to do to help."

Angel grabbed her purse and rushed out to meet them. When she arrived, the eternal hive of beggars stretched far and wide around the concrete columns. Easter always sparked parishioners to flood the gods and ask for clemency. She stood so far away that she couldn't even see the gods' three-strand magic through the window. When she tried to push her way through, she found herself weakened by the lack of follicles. It was then that she realized how much strength her hair held. Angel struggled even harder, throwing all her might against the sea of poorheads. She finally made so much noise that the gods stopped and gave her their attention.

"Where have you come from? What do you seek?"

"My edges . . . they are gone. Tell me how to get them back," she exclaimed.

The gods laughed.

"John the Conqueror with all the Devil's daughter's magic couldn't plow those edges back!"

The raucous laughter spread like an outbreak throughout the crowd. Angel shrank, trying to shield her hairline with her hands, inching away in embarrassment. Just as she was reaching the back of the sea of mockery, she heard a whistle.

She followed the whistle deep into the back alleys. It curved her around the nightclubs and past the fish market. Before long, Angel found herself utterly turned around in a part of town she had never been to before. The whistle grew louder and louder until it was an all-consuming hum. She fell to her knees grasping her ears. When the ringing stopped, she found she had been transported to the home of the Sangoma. Here, the old woman danced in a bright gold scarf in the smoke of moxa and herb.

"Where am I? How did I get here?" Angel asked.

"I heard your crying near the temple. And I saw your head from the stratosphere."

Angel cringed, attempting to hide the barren field.

"I have the answers you seek," said the Sangoma.

"You know how to convince my edges to come back?"

"It is easier than you think."

"Tell me, tell me," begged Angel.

The Sangoma hovered over a counter full of vials holding foul-colored liquids. She pulled three off the shelf. Then she grabbed a wooden bowl from a lower rack.

"You must need your beauty more than you want it. It must ravage you from the core. Tell me, does it?"

"Yes!" Angel cried out, as the Sangoma poured vial after vial into a dark slush.

"Then drink this."

The Sangoma presented a wooden cup, no bigger than her hands. Angel could smell the bubbling concoction from across the room. Its nose-singeing aroma causing her stomach to churn, the Sangoma pushing the cup closer and closer to her face.

"Drink!"

Angel was out of options. She pressed the cup to her lips and swallowed chunk after chunk of the brown mystery liquid. Before long, the sleep began to take over. She fought hard but quickly found herself even weaker than before. The Sangoma approached with a mirror in her hand. The last sight Angel saw, before passing out, was that of her and the Sangoma's reflection in the mirror blurring to a fog.

When she woke up, the Sangoma was gone. She was groggy, and the room felt like it was spinning. Angel clawed her way across the floor to grab the mirror to see if it had worked. The reflection started as a ball of light, quickly clearing its shine to reveal Angel's bald head. Angel screamed. Her vulnerability for all to see, now caught in her throat, unable to climb out. She stood and stumbled to the window to look for the Sangoma. Nothing. To the door? Nothing. Down the street? A hint of the Sangoma's gold scarf trailed around a beautiful woman's neck. Her hair flowy and familiar. The Sangoma now embodied a young woman who laughed and danced about, flicking her long, straight locks in the wind. Angel was furious. She began barreling after the Sangoma to get her hair back. People in the street quickly began to jeer. Laughing and pointing and making all sorts of jokes. The Sangoma saw Angel coming and took to a foot race. Both women snowballing through boutiques, crashing through bookstores, leaving a slew of destruction. The Sangoma turned down a long street only to find it a dead end.

"Give me my hair!" Angel demanded.

The Sangoma searched for a way out, only to see Angel getting closer and closer. Then the piercing whistle. Angel, no longer with the shield of any hair to muffle the shrill, collapsed on the ground. The ringing ended to reveal the Sangoma as nothing more than a pile of skin at the feet of her edges. Angel cowered beneath them confused. The edges took to voice, one loud and clear.

"Now you know what it feels like to be ignored. For no one to see the beauty you can hold. How did it feel to be forced to bend to another's control? To be turned into something you aren't?"

Angel was dumbfounded. She found her heart skipping like a scratched CD. Angel begged for forgiveness. She denied the gods and promised to turn over a new leaf. Her edges were hesitant; Angel made peppermint oil promises and vowed to protect them at all costs, until they agreed to give her another chance to prove herself.

The next morning, her head was a field of fuzz. Each strand testing the limitations of trust inch by inch, hour by hour. By the time dawn broke after the next crescent moon, Angel's head was a vibrant bush. When she rose before the mirror, she was blinded by the sheen of her glistening afro.

When Angel passed the temple this time, the gods were in awe of her globe of wonder. They dropped their fairy dust and magic shears to gawk in the window. The poorheads in line gasped at the strength and wonder. The gods begged that she would show them her ways, but Angel remembered their cruelty. The gods knew they must come together and craft an offering to Angel as an apology. They decided on a golden pick, one whose handle was fashioned justly into a fist. They gifted it to Angel and changed her name to Afrodite: god of wondrous globe and natural beauty.

Now she reigns high and mighty above the thrones of heat alongside the other Crop Gods. Always in full glow, edges always divinely laid.

Maybe her throne was what taught my mother how to find God in herself. Maybe it is only a fragment. For what is it that a mirror measures but a slim piece of you? One we give so much attention but in and of itself is so shallow.

Perhaps this story is how I learned to love myself fiercely. Her throne, a metaphor. Though I am no longer one to lean into comparisons. Maybe this one is for our children. For the children that become ours by some other way. For the children inside us that never get out. That learn to tell stories, like striking book after book of matches, just for warmth.

If you hide long enough,
Even you won't be able
To find yourself.

He May Not Come When
You Want Him

I don't know a library that isn't a church. A sanctuary of stories no less holy than another. Even Lucifer had his tale. And religiously, every week, my mother would take me to church.

The Riverside public church sat near the middle of the Empire's historic district. More than a holder of old wood, must, and an up-close view of the mountains that surrounded it, it held the language of the creaking spines. It was a refuge for the homeless when the weather got too cold and a haven for the poor who couldn't afford dial-up internet or the newest IBM computer, like the one my father brought home for us to play *The Oregon Trail* and *Prince of Persia*. It sat at the base of a valley. The large, tan stucco walls seemed to survive every sandstorm the Santa Ana winds learned to throw. The main entrance shared concrete with the old mission building. A sweeping bell sat in earshot, marking every hour passed with an urgency to seek out more understanding.

We were homeschooled, so Tuesdays became our holy day. We would slip away from watching *I, Claudius* or reading *The People Could Fly* in our history unit to sit out under the church's giant Chinese pagoda and eat brown-sack communion from my mother's oversize purse. We marveled at the red curved roof that was guarded by giant ivory foo dogs; they seemed to make the place safe. So safe in fact that my brother and I could wander through the multiple floors of knowledge unaccompanied without disturbing my mother. There was peace for all of us there in the large stacks of books. Everything from Psalms to Shakespeare, but my most sacred place was made just for children.

There was a long elevator ride to get up to the Children's Place. It sat closer to God in that way. And when those metal doors pulled open, the bustle of children's laughter was a holy resound. It was the only place in church that there was no expectation of quiet, though we rarely wanted to be louder than the Great Librarian. She had been there before the church had walls or a roof to stand under. Heaven-picked, she was omniscience embodied. Knew where to find every book, what to recommend, when you were ready for another circle time, even made space for the quiet of us to pull curated bags of books and tapes to pop into our

Walkmans or a borrowed radio and hear it all in another voice. She knew her limitations, but she showed us all that we didn't have any.

She was small and missable in any other instance, but during circle time the wisdom radiated from her like a beacon. And every few hours, she would transform the center rug into a boat in the sea of the room's center and call all the children to come to her. Her large brown hands would unfold some hardbound scripture as she settled in, crisscross applesauce, in the center of the room. We would gather to her, that low and lulling voice reverberating wonder, telling us many things, parables of life.

The Parable of the Gardeners

Two neighboring women went out to start their gardens, the way a coming Good Friday dictates. They both began to clear the earth, making sure it was ripe for planting, and after days of tilling, the women sat down to decide what to plant. Before them lay two options: the fragrant blooms of Hope or the sprawling ivy of Fear. Some said growing Hope was a young woman's game, because, while it was the most captivating choice, it took years to sprout. One might think it dead and plant something else, only to be startled when one spring, Hope blooms eternal. Fear, on the other hand, was instant. Within days of planting it, its small, winding vines would begin creeping out from the rich soil. The swelling stems would mutate before your eyes, doubling in size every day. If left unpruned, Fear would choke out everything in its path, including the house itself.

The first gardener decided to take the route of quick results, scattering seeds of Fear throughout her entire plot. The second gardener thought herself a patient woman. After much reflection she decided to scatter Hope by the handful. Both women would rise daily before the sun to re-create the sky's dew from large tin water cans that they carried out, heavily laden, from the house. But on the third day, things began to change.

The Fear-gardener began to see the fruits of her labor. Tiny green leaves began their spring emergence. By the next day, there were enough vines across the plot's face to impersonate a vibrant lawn. The Hope-gardener just watered the empty dirt, transforming her plot into a mud-drenched swamp. She hoped to see something miraculous but knew her crop may take just a little longer to become visible to the naked eye. She fertilized and watered, and watered and waited on the sun, expecting nothing more than what would come.

By the next week, the Fear-gardener's plot was abounding with life. The vines were now so long that they began tangling the trees. With little watering, they seemed to be insatiable, growing in between stones, over fallen stumps, around animals' dens that sat too still. The Fear-gardener found that pruning took much of her morning, but rising with a purpose to pare things back every day was more satisfying than waiting on what may never come. The Hope-gardener sat steady on her back porch, watching the day shift to night, pruning the unwanted weeds to make room for something bigger.

And this went on for two seasons. The Fear-gardener toiling with the wall's encroaching vines, and the Hope-gardener staring at the maddening field of nothingness. Until one day, the Fear-gardener took pity on her neighbor. She showed up on her back porch with a gift: a small snip taken from her glorious yard.

"I have watched you struggle," she said to her neighbor, "and I worry that you will drive yourself mad with waiting. Will you bet on what may never come when all of this green is already here? Take this small bit, may it bring you some comfort, something to see live in your hopeless field."

The Hope-gardener hesitated to take the offering. She still believed something would bloom, but the years between had been hard. She struggled to eat with very little crops and had little to sell to the nearby market. She didn't want to admit she was losing faith that the plot would ever green. She knew, deep inside, that something was still there, but the strange sprout enchanted her. It beamed with life before her eyes. It began shifting and growing right there in her hands. That's when the bargaining with herself began:

"What if I build a small planter at the far end of the plot? I could have something to watch thrive, and still keep room for all my Hope. And if it ever gets too big, I can just pare it back."

This logic sounded reasonable. She didn't have to sacrifice one for the other. Her plot was big enough for both. So she spent one Sunday morning building a box from two-by-fours and planter bricks to house the plant that was now almost as big as she was, despite her constant pruning. She used all of her might to haul the vine far out to the end of the plot and plant it in a shallow bed to limit its reach. By sunset, she was exhausted and stumbled back into the house.

The next morning, the Hope-gardener rose to a shrill scream and the sound of glass breaking. She ran outside to see that one of the Fear-gardener's vines had grown straight through the window and was now reaching for the leg of her dining room table. The Fear-gardener had been startled and quickly retrieved her shears to cut it back and put it in its rightful place. This intrusion made the Hope-gardener consider her own plot. She ran to her yard to see that the Fear she planted, just the night before, had already cracked through the wood and staked its claim directly in the soil. She quickly retrieved her shears and chopped down the entire plant before it had any more room to grow. But what is planted will eventually thrive.

The next morning, the Hope-gardener woke to water her field in a new rededication to her original plan. When her water finally reached the soil, she was surprised to find a minuscule mound breaking forth. This was not like anything she had ever seen. No, this was a blue-veined delicacy that had been pushing forth, quiet and unassuming. Here, where she only longed, Hope was springing. The Hope-gardener was so taken by her new crop, she didn't notice the distant creep of green out on the horizon. She brought her new blossoms banana water and sprinkled Epsom salt everywhere to make sure all her dreams were given their chance to thrive. But the ivy grew closer.

After a few days, her Hope had petals. Soft blue buds shaped like hearts that were one ounce of sunlight away from full bloom. That's when the Hope-gardener finally lifted her eyes and noticed the field. The stretching, inching, threatening field of Fear that now came like a tsunami's wave to threaten all the Hope she had waited a lifetime to have. She didn't know what to do. How would she beat back so much Fear in such little time?

The Hope-gardener ran to the Fear-gardener's house to ask for help. Surely she would know how to contain this beast she spent day and night forcing into submission. But when she arrived at what used to be the Fear-gardener's porch, she realized just how much time had passed since her last visit. The Fear-gardener's house, if that's what you chose to call it, was just a shell. A box of curated vine where every window was an entry point. Remnants of a refrigerator, stove, stand mixer. Couches and hallways were suffocated with the sprawl of green that choked out every inch of the home. And there, among the foliage, a foot? A pair of swallowed shears?

Dread filled every inch of her body. She pushed and pulled at the throbbing vines trying to reach the familiar legs that no longer twitched in the wreckage, but Fear's stomach had already been satisfied. And as the last of her friend's body disappeared into a swell of green, she knew there was no one and no way to stop what was next.

The Hope-gardener returned to the sound of inevitable danger swallowing the plot a foot at a time. She watched as every Hope she had was tangled and twisted and suffocated from its roots. A sea of decapitated blue buds in a swath of green violence. And before long, her house was gone too.

Whoever has an ear, let him hear. And whoever has a tongue, let him tell. That God lives in many vessels and faith in even more derivations. That a body may be a temple, a building, but only if you grow the right story in it. And, oh, what kinds of stories I have made a sanctuary for. How I have toiled to make my body new.

I Can Show You Better Than I Can Tell You

Church was nothing like St. John's. No, at St. John's we only knew how to compete. The elegant cross fought the brick-and-wood building on the corner lot. The steeple looked down over the rest of the Empire's valley as if it was positioned for judgment. The large movie marquee boasted the title of Sunday's upcoming sermon like a new release, fighting with every other worship hall in the valley for any believers willing to switch teams. Then, there was inside.

The brown wooden ledger of last week's attendance sat at the entrance, prodding us like a new world record that begged to be shattered. Maroon-bound songbooks fought for pew space between the funeral fans and the tissue boxes. The swamp cooler fought the rising summer temperatures and always lost. Butterscotch women quarreled over the front rows, taking up all the sight line with their broad-rim Easter hats. And me, well, I was always fighting every other god for my father's attention.

My father was a giant. Six foot seven and the wingspan of a mighty eagle. His shoulders were broad, and his brute strength made him superhero-untouchable, with the Superman curl in his hair to match. The strong and silent Black man whose bronze skin glistened transparent against the blue veins I traced up his legs on the beach or during our camping trips to Dana Point. His eyes were my mother's kryptonite, green with specks of light, just like T's. He sat at Pastor James's right side every Sunday. Just an arm's length away from my mother and the two squirrely children who tried to stay seated in the front pew. And when my mother was called upon to bless the heavenlies with her voice in the choir, we sat with friends or non-blood family or godparents or were kept close in the eyes of the white gloves, who policed the aisles looking for loud children sneaking gum before being dismissed from their parents. My mother says I would wait until she was deep in the soprano section to do cartwheels on the front row or bear crawl under the sloping pews to make my way to my father. Even as a toddler, I would crawl my way up the steps of the pulpit to his feet, where I would fall asleep in his lap for the entire service. There was something about the strongbox of my father's arms that made me feel indestructible. That was, until I was too old to justify staying in them.

At one measure of time or another, all children would be too old to stay in service. They would be ushered from their parents' eyes in a single-file line to the concrete basement. Down there, behind the large partitions, the younger children experimented with coloring Jesus's skin various shades of purple and learned how lions and whales exist to show us God's wrathful love. The older of us, those my brother's age, found themselves practicing Bible drills or memorizing the exhaustive sixty-six-book library that struggled to answer every question they had—at least in Brother Chestnut's hands. He tried to keep them engaged, betting all his money on their inability to remember verses or find all the names of the Old Testament titles in word puzzles. I was later one of the few children who taught him the dangers of promising money to motivated children with hungry intellects. And while there was a certain lovely and predictable chaos, much of it was us buying time until the duplex cookies and diabetes punch welcomed the new converts and let us free to scuff our Sunday shoes climbing trees or turning flips on the metal railings out front.

On Baptism Sundays, all time seemed to be even more

endless. Our descension would be delayed as we sat along our parents and cheered as people emerged from the watery grave that was cut into the floor of the pulpit. The way my father explained it, we had to die in order to be closer to God. Jesus did it and this was our turn. And my childlike rationale took everything literally. I would watch those Sunday rituals closely, like a crime show, trying to piece together all the clues. Pastor James would enter the water first, dressed in a long white robe that seemed to cling to his dark skin upon entry. He would start with a story, one he told so many times, all of us had it memorized:

Then Jesus came from Galilee to John at the Jordan to be baptized by him. And John tried to prevent Him, saying, "I need to be baptized by You, and are You coming to me?"

But Jesus answered and said to him, "Permit it to be so now, for thus it is fitting for us to fulfill all righteousness." Then he allowed Him.

When He had been baptized, Jesus came up immediately from the water; and behold, the heavens were opened to Him, and He saw the Spirit of God descending like a dove and alighting upon Him. And suddenly a voice came from Heaven, saying, "This is My beloved Son, in whom I am well pleased."

Then the newest converts would walk the green mile and line up. Each one descending into the water to recite a few words, only to be dunked backward by Pastor James's forceful hand on their chest like a resuscitation paddle. They would rebound with a violent gasp as if they were breathing new oxygen, before the room erupted in applause at the near drowning. After this, they were new and somehow better? At six, I wasn't exactly sure how it all worked, but I was positive that I didn't want the alternative. The one that Pastor James, the other deacons, and my father all mentioned at the conclusion of every service and every prayer:

Let those all find Jesus and allow Him into their heart, lest they be condemned to a lake of fire where there will be weeping and gnashing of teeth.

I wasn't sure what gnashing was, but it made my mouth hurt. And if desert summers were any indication of my ability to survive a fiery eternity, I needed to make some other plans.

So one Sunday, when our teacher Mrs. Donna was getting us ready to rejoin our parents for the benediction, I mentioned to her that I didn't want to burn to death. Her brown eyes filled with joy. She explained that all I had to do was make room in my heart and let Jesus in. I wasn't sure how He would fit, but I trusted that if my mother and father could do it, I could do it too. She marched me up the stairs, but this time, instead of taking me to my mother, she stood me at the other end of a long aisle facing the pulpit and my father.

When they cast out the choice, the everlasting competition between eternal damnation and sprawling mansions, I made a decision. I let go of Mrs. Donna's hand and stumbled down the large, expanding aisle toward my father's open arms. Tears began to run down his reddening cheeks as his heart swooned with pride. The room erupted in claps and screams. The butterscotch women waved their white handkerchiefs, the white gloves paused their scowls for brief hallelujahs, and Pastor James squatted down to place a microphone at my mouth to confess to the entire room that I was sure about my decision. And while I wasn't sure what all I was committing to, the look in my father's eyes made me sure I was doing the right thing.

On the next Baptism Sunday, they dressed me in white graveclothes. Momma Gloria, my godmother, was assigned to hold my hand as I approached the water. I stood in the eaves with my mind on fast-forward as I stared down into the water-filled pit. I could see it now: Pastor James would call me down into the water, he would extend his hand to receive all of the might I heard God had when He struck down the tower of Babel. He would smite his hand down against my chest. I would be submerged, and he would hold me under so long that life would leave clean out of my body. Then he would disappear. I didn't know how to swim, and no one would hear me gasping for air when they closed the floor back over my filling lungs and resumed service. By the time Sister Butts kicked off her shoes and made it to full dance in the pew to the choir's B selection, I would be gone. I just knew it. Pastor James would preach an entire sermon, dancing on my watery grave, before Jesus ever came to revive me or my father was able to break me out.

By the time it was my turn to descend, they told me I had to cross my arms over my chest the way they do casket-clothed corpses. I had seen it once before. I had no desire to play with Death, even then. I refused. As Momma Gloria tried to nudge me down into the water, my parents watching in utter pride, I tried to flee. I pulled at her white gown, I tried to turn around, but Pastor James already had my hand. He caught the Holy Ghost's mighty smite; then it descended with all power in his hand into my chest. I plummeted into the water, holding my nose, thinking that would give me a few more seconds of escape. But before I could assess the best way to fight back, I was on the upside of the water and the congregation was in full cheer. I was pulled out and taken out a side exit; Momma Gloria hugged me with tears streaming down her face. Then she asked me how I felt. I guess I was supposed to feel warm or shiny or somehow more made in His image, but I was just cold and wet. And when I dried off, my arms were still wiry, my legs still lanky, but I had survived being reborn. I hoped that would count for something. At least in my father's eyes.

In so many ways we seek to be something. To grow up like a premonition. But we are our father's daughters too. And for every inch our mothers give us in sight, our fathers gift us every harvest of speech.

More important than my father's arms was the rattling bass of his voice. It would crawl from deep down in his diaphragm to rumble in worship. It was the same voice that met me in the evening's bedside. There, my father taught me how to speak in story. I mastered it late at night, in the few stolen moments I had between his arrival from work and my drifting off to sleep. He would haul some big book onto my blanket-wrapped legs, deep in the safety of my yellow-walled room. I would hug my Glo Worm and shine the light from its pea-child face over every larger-than-life word. My mother always said he was doing too much, as every character crawled out of his mouth in a different voice. He was possessed by narration. Anansi lived in his lungs, Brer Bear in his diaphragm, I was sure. Every character inhabiting his body, neighbor to Jesus, and he let them turn his mouth into a full stage. It was one of a few practices with him I could be sure of: pancakes on Saturday morning, bike rides that afternoon, and nightly stories.

So on the night that adulting got in the way of religion, a night made for long commutes and even longer apologies, my mother tried to fill in. She read the words but didn't know the language. These were not her stories to tell. Each character was flat and sounded like her and wanted to point out every plot hole I never saw before because I was so captivated by every note of my father's internal harmony. She offered kisses. She offered hugs. She offered excuses, but I wanted my father to speak to me.

I lay there in the silence for what seemed like hours, staring into the glow of the dark stars that littered my ceiling, until finally crawling out of bed. The house was dark, all but a single light that flickered over the stove. My mother would leave it on so that my father wouldn't have to enter a darkened house. I snuck down the hallway near the vents where the builders stashed their beer cans when constructing our manufactured oasis in the desert. At night, you could hear them rattle when the heat turned on. I made my way to the landing of the staircase, which dumped out in two directions, toward my room and toward the front door. There was no way we would miss each other from there. I leaned on the wall nearby and waited to intercept my father when he returned. Hoped he would get there soon. I waited and waited, until the small flickering light became only a pinhole in the dark and the clinking cans became the only voice echoing through the house.

The next moment, my eyes opened and I was back in my room. The sun was shining and my father was nowhere to be found. I had no idea how I had been transported there. All I knew was that, when I needed my father to speak, he abandoned me. I searched the entire house for him, checked closet crawl spaces, roller-skate closets, I even looked in their forbidden bedroom. I found only my mother, scrubbing the bathtub with the green grit of Comet, singing herself a song. When I demanded she make my father show himself, she said he was already gone to work.

I sulked all day in my father's absence. Resentment crawling through every extremity until the moon started its ascension and the front door creaked with a familiar chime. Today, there was no running into his arms. No sweet cheek kisses as he palmed a pair of golden bomber earrings for me to collect. I wanted no pleasantries. Just answers.

I guess my folded arms and gnarled nose were enough to speak volumes of my discontent. My father, in the way only he knew how, scooped me up and put me on his knee. He touched my nose with his knuckle and I tried not to break into a smile. He had some explaining to do.

"Why didn't you come home last night?" I demanded. "I waited for you and you never showed up. You were supposed to be here to read to me."

His eyes glowed under my accusations and his smile grew wider.

"When I came home, you were asleep on the landing. I picked you up and put you back in bed. Would you have rather I'd woken you up?"

Sheepishly, my arms lost tension and my head bowed. He slid his knuckle under my chin, tickled until no squirming or wiggling could contain my laughter. And then all the waiting, all the silence, was a millisecond lost in my father's hand. And he was here, just in time to read to me again.

Hope may not come when you want it, but its timeliness may be the only way I know to speak of my father. What a dangerous deity. Hope, begging you to risk all on its fickle arrival. It asks you to bet your happiness on a vision of life, possible blessing/possible swindle. For Faith can quickly change from the substance of things hoped for to the alibi of a crime unseen.

My father had a way of fixing everything with his words. When couples were troubled in their marriages, one conversation with him seemed to pull them from the edge of divorce. When my mother warned that all my eating would make me "as big as a house," his reminder that my big feet were made to support a full body brought me back into balance. But there was a brewing conflict in our home that beseeched my father more often than any other: the constant uprise between my teenage brother and my mother.

Maybe they fought so much because they were so alike. Spitting image in skin tone, passionate hotheads who were both grieving the working version of my father that still stained pictures of the three of them on K Street. By the time we moved deeper into the Empire's desert, my father's forced retirement made him more of a fleeting wind, coming and going at the beck and call of his needy parishioners. And while he had explained, upon accepting his calling, that

"God was calling us all in this," no one knew how absent he would become from our home. And misery's plight for company didn't build comradery as well as Silence's anger built contempt. My mother and her firstborn spent their days together planting land mines to protect themselves from the hurt, only to injure us all in the process.

On long days after school, I would tumble home to crash on the brown recliner couch and watch *Tiny Toon Adventures* or *Animaniacs*. I finished most of my homework early, and the TV offered a necessary distraction from the brooding feud around me. I was too young to drive away and too old to pretend the tension didn't exist, so I latched onto *Pinky and the Brain* in an effort to hatch a best-made plan of escaping unscathed. This day, my father happened to be home. I'm not sure if it was between shifts serving as the fire department's chaplain or a sprinkled moment before he headed out to teach a Bible study at the convalescent hospital where his mother counted her last rounds, but my father sat in the back bedroom far away from the action.

My brother joined me for an after-school laugh, stretching his full adolescent body across the love seat until parts of him dangled off either end. My mother had her own task in reorganizing our mini church that took up an entire wall of our home. Every home should have its own temple. Ours sat stocked with a full Encyclopædia Britannica set that I am sure my mother bought from a TV advertisement at some insomniac hour. There were copies of *National Geographic*, with flat-breasted women whose nipples hung south of their belly buttons, next to my favorite Black royalty series that taught me about Black inventors and Black scientists. It had everything. And my mother tapped into the Great Librarian in all of us, curating age-appropriate recommendations and filling in every Black gap that public school may have missed. She pulled books and built towers of new offerings on the floor across from us. We all moved in such seamless silence across our open-concept living space. My brother and I in sparse moments of laughter in the sunken living room, the rhythm of my mother's book-stacking, and nothing from my distant father.

That is, until my mother asked my brother for something. I'm not sure what she needed because I was too engrossed in "Wakko's America." But before it ended, the volume of voices started to raise. It seemed my mother had asked my brother to do something for a third time, and instead of just doing it, he launched a grenade in lip smack at our mother's feet. She stood and asked the answerless question, "Are you getting smart with me?" To which my brother responded with an eye roll. He thought she would just ignore the assault, but my mother had had enough. I am not sure if it was the pressure of raising two children on her own while my father served as surrogate savior or the pure frustration of having no other adult to speak to, but this infraction was enough to send her into combat mode. A trigger that reverberated through every spy tendency. And before I had a chance to duck, my mother, the sniper, was already taking aim.

I was now fully aware of the danger I sat in. On either side of me, attitudes heightened and tempers flared. My brother's indifference to my mother's request and my mother's insistence on being heard, each offering no sign of relenting. And then the gauntlet dropped. She rolled up her sleeves and all her spy training came full frontal lobe.

She said, "Oh, so you want to get smart with me? I will show you smart!"

She picked up a medium-size book from the stack and cocked it back and fired the loaded clip. It shot past my head and missed my brother by centimeters. A warning shot. She was toying with him. We both knew what she was capable of.

He jumped over the couch and sent back an insult: "Mom! Stop acting crazy!"

"Crazy? Oh, I will show you crazy!"

And a larger, felt-bound book ripped through the air, just missing my leg and landing on my brother's side of the couch. He jumped up, and she saw him in brief ascension. She aimed again, now yelling something about showing him how smart he was. Encyclopedia volume 1. *A Midsummer Night's Dream*. A collection of Martin Luther King's speeches. He bobbed and weaved as I slipped down onto the ground to barrel crawl to the nearby hallway and head for my parents' room.

I wondered if my father was asleep. If he had heard them. Why he hadn't emerged to stop the onslaught. When I opened his door, I realized that he was fully aware, as he lay across his bed watching *Matlock*. I stared at him, hoping he would offer me some rationale or in some way speak a storm calm. That he would save me the way Peter was saved, but it is easier to forget what you cannot see. He just turned up the TV until the story line masked the undertone of interspersed screams and thuds. I sat on the edge of the bed for a long moment hoping this was a space of refuge. But if I learned anything, it's that hiding smoke does nothing to the fire.

Maybe this was what happens when you spend years conjuring up everyone's truths with nowhere to put your own. To be an open book, with so many alternate endings to choose from, gives room for some dangerous outcomes. And in the same way my father moved in his own time and came to his own silence, something just as sinister was coming to me.

When you're grown from gunpowder,
You have no choice
but to be the bomb.

Dusting the Child from Our Bodies

I have resolved that the child in me didn't have enough time. As if time is ever of any consequence when immortality lies in the balance. But time is merely a measurement of how many lots we have cast for what we would change. Uneven odds, they say. And though my youth was surrounded by loving arms, I still find myself lost in Nostalgia's gaze. Wishing I could turn myself inside out. Take back the moment I knew how treacherous things would become. Back when my father's mother spun me a web of safety next to a cautionary tale of what could be.

She always told us it could happen. Out there on Elva Ave., deep under the south-central wing of seraphim, where the street boasted a quaint Pleasantville quiet and the neighbors knew everyone by name. Grandma and Grandpa moved to the City after the war to start a new life with my father. As it goes, the neighborhood built up around them. The Dixons moved in on the corner, and they became quick friends. The Manns settled in at the other end in the blue house whose back was never blind to anything. Their house anchored the block. The brick steps led to a large wooden door with crystal inlays on either side. The Malbec rose bushes flanking the yard afforded just enough space for duck and cover during hide-and-seek. Pastures of green lush held our bare feet in the summer. All but still waters there.

T's daughter, Tyeisha, and I would spend hours turning our bodies into dancing shadows in the dry heat. Two bodies of the same age and similar size, born worlds apart to feuding mothers. Mothers who loved us with all that they had, even when what they had wasn't much. This place was a neutral zone where childhood sat heavy and saw us like peas in a timeline of pods that wanted nothing but play. This was the soil where we built mudpies, and told stories, and found how many layers were in a yellow onion by peeling it back, fleshy scales littering the yard in translucence. Where we hid from our mothers until the point of their terror. This alluring oasis in the middle of territory we didn't know belonged to everybody but us.

Grandma always warned that the pops we heard at New Year's, Fourth of July, a random weekend evening, were not always fireworks. But in an effort to pad us with safety, my grandfather would rise as the third-shifters closed out and gather all the dented cans, seasonal shelf items, and bruised produce the grocery stores didn't want. Then anyone could come to our house and take what they needed from the makeshift market spread across the dining room floor. We'd pocket marshmallow Peeps well into the summer and eat handfuls of Christmas Crunch in the spring, never worrying about expiration dates, because here time stood so still that we could celebrate each breath and laugh together. We never saw the rumored violence. We never felt the encroaching fear.

Until today.

Tyeisha and I are ready. We gather all the purple jump ropes from the game room and head to the front yard. We spread the ropes wide. I haven't mastered double Dutch, and there is no one else to turn the ropes, so we stick to single jumping on the faded hopscotch we drew yesterday.

"I bet you can't beat my record."

A glove smacked clean across the face in the perfect etiquette of a duel. The clacking of ABC barrettes and multicolored beads punctuate our laughter. We are taking turns seeing who can outdo the other in consecutive bounces without a misstep. At the height of the jump, everything is a blur, unbridled motion and tippy-toe carelessness. If we're careful, we crisscross the rope under our feet, turn backward. We're all childhood distraction. We miss the first warning.

Tyeisha is jumping now. A car enters, driving Sunday-afternoon slow in the middle of the week. Four men sit in the car, two in front, two in back. Their eyes are covered with dark sunglasses. They don't regard the light. Around their chins hang bandanas, vibrant, red—the polar opposite of the Manns' house on the corner. They creep at such a pace that Tyeisha has time to beat my record and then hers again. I watch them take the corner deeper into the neighborhood, away from the main road.

She hands me the rope. It's my turn. I know I must jump like my life depends on it. I set in with the rhythm: the click-clack keeps time like a djembe. The rope brushes against the pavement, then arches its body over my head and rushes back to my feet. Strappy inertia, all muscles and potential energy. I hear the screech.

The first pop, New Year's Eve familiar. A little girl, too far down the street to know my name, screams. We, in and out of our own bodies: an inalienable intelligence. And the fireworks: purple rope, green grass, gray pavement, rainbow beads, red roses, brown thorns, green grass, green grass, green grass.

The voice of a gun is a recognizable terror, like a mother calling her kids in out of the dark. I learned early, if you ever hear it, level your body as close to the ground as possible. Make yourself invisible. Most people shoot straight. They don't aim beneath what they can easily see.

There is a second screech, and the familiar car is a blur. I look for Tyeisha, who is flush against the earth. Her back still. In flutter. We wait until the street has reset to the familiar hum of faint highways and distant hopscotch. Before the sirens. We pull ourselves from the earth and gather up the ropes, dusting the child from our bodies. Fully aware of what fear may come, there is no more time left to play. In the space of a single day. Grown.

It is easy to perceive that threats are everywhere when you are a moving target. It is easy to unpack yourself as a victim when you want to hold on to the version of you before the pain. But I had reconciled, even then, that play left room for loss. Do not be sad for that. Our hands give and take. No hesitation. This is the natural order of things. I did not realize how internal the questioning would become until much later. How the fear gentrifies everywhere, looking for a way to get in.

I was ten, entering the doors of Star Burger after my mother lifted the ban on eating there due to their support of apartheid. She said we wouldn't support racism. I just wanted my waffle fries. Once Nelson Mandela made his way home, we sat under the single smiling star pulsing in a strip mall in the desert, happy to be back to order our bacon western cheeseburgers and the crunch of perfectly fried potato hashtags. There was a long line when we arrived. My brother and father told my mom their orders before slipping out the back door to the patio to hold our table. I danced eagerly, sliding my body under and over the chain-link divider like it was a game of Chinese jump rope that I just couldn't kill. My mother tried to reel in my body from bumping into other patrons. She reminded me that we were not born from grace. Maybe the child had not fully left my body, but I was twice the size I should be. An emerging townhome, in my mother's eyes. I wanted so much to find my own gangly independence, and my mother felt me pulling. So once all was paid for, she tasked me with holding the plastic tent number and waiting by the long bar under the pickup sign for our order. She joined my father and brother outside, where the sun was just warm enough to cut the chill of fall.

I danced around, imagining that the floor was made of lava, that the black tiles fell into a helpless abyss and the white tiles held the safety of shaky cliffs. I fed the Tamagotchi that Monique gave me in one of our rare interactions, even though I never wanted to play mother prematurely the way she and T had. Both becoming parents before gaining graduation caps. I was still a child myself. I played a dozen songs in my head and sang them all backward, and the wait seemed endless.

They eventually called my number. There were two trays and drinks for four, but I was sure my mile-long arms and flat chest would serve me well. I balanced the trays on my forearms and the drinks triangled together between my fingers. Then I started my approach toward the glass door in the back. People watched in awe as, step after step, the cups of orange soda and cola sloshed back and forth but never tipped. All were so impressed that no one offered to help. Not the freckle-faced employees, not the mother with three kids of her own, screaming for them to stay in their seats in the back corner, not even the man who watched me the entire time I was in line creating my own dance club.

I noticed him when we first walked in. He sat alone at a table near the door reading his paper, glancing up occasionally and then quickly disappearing behind the text again. He was enamored with me. Each stare longer than the last. By the time the fries and drinks joined my act, he was entranced with my off-kilter teetering. I made my way toward him. I could see my family on the back porch under the metal umbrella's red-and-white sanctuary. I shifted and shifted as I tried to find a third hand to push the bar of the door open into the fall air—any extra appendages, prehistoric relic members. Then, an idea.

I turned my back around and hurled my butt into the bar, sending the door flying into the wind. As it opened, the crowd seemed unmoved by all my quickening genius. All but the paper man by the door. Who folded back the entertainment section and howled, "So that's what all that ass is for?" loud enough for the entire restaurant to stop and examine all my ten-year-old Hottentot exotica.

I cut my eyes hard at him. The way my mom did the first time I said a curse word in front of her. Hard enough to make the room begin to shake. His body gave over into violent convulsions. The families at the tables around him began snatching their children close. His hands radiated, his chest bulged, the ceiling fought to hold his rising back.

By now, the nearbys had taken to full sprints. Then his face peeled away and before me stood Acirema, the greatest warrior spirit. Born of a restless dust devil, he made the brown projects cower with his white gaze, the strength of twelve settlers in one hand and the brawn of four grandmothers who won their rounds with Death in the other. The star-spangled spitfire soul slayer. His legs stretched high and wide, his stovepipe hat splintering through the roof and up to the heavens. He began to violently sling tables and soda machines at the wall.

The land before us became a fast-food desert. Acirema's sharpened finger brandished as a sword. One the length of three Cadillacs and the sharpness of the Crop Gods' tongues. He pointed at me. As if to initiate an ultimate duel. I leapt behind the counter, spilling all the food onto the checkered floor. I made the cashier give me her red hat as a helmet, and I used one of the serving trays as a shield. Acirema, like legend says, alternated finger slices and exhales so rancid that he could level an entire army with just the smell of his breath. I held my air and looked for a way to fight back. I searched my pockets but found only a pack of sunflower seeds. They would have to do. I loaded my mouth with a handful and hopped over the pickup station. Acirema saw me and cocked the large blade to come down on me, but I was too fast. The padding of my hips softened the slide as I glided across the floor and waited for my moment. Acirema inhaled deeply to power a deadly belt and I machine-gun spat every last seed from the barrel of my mouth. Most missed, but one arched with perfection and landed in the slack-jawed mouth of Acirema.

Instantly, he knew what I had done. The salt from the seed spread across his tongue and down the backside of his throat until a cough ensued. He tried to drown it out by slurping the exploded soda from the sea that had formed near the entrance, but that only made the seed hungry for soil. Within seconds, Acirema felt the roots protruding from his stomach, up through his lungs. Desperate to stop the spread, he charged through the wall and turned the restaurant into rubble. He began to grab clumps of parking lot, swallowing the rocks that tumbled down from the nearby mountains, in the hope that they would bury the sprout that now leafed polyps from his nose and sought to invade his head. He swallowed more and more, until he fell to the ground, too heavy to fight. Acirema tried to claw the plant out. He thrashed about, destroying cars and buildings. I knew he wouldn't stop until it was free or everything around him ceased to exist.

I did what I had to. I bent Acirema's long finger back with both hands until it broke free. Then I approached, swinging it as high and as hard as I could. It landed in the middle of his lips, cracking his skull from jaw to crown. Bursting the polyps. But there was no blood. Instead, doubts, like a horde of horseflies in incantation, filled the sky above Acirema's ruptured head. Looking for noses to invade, they found me. And I was not light enough to fly away.

A Dead Bee Can Still Sting

I didn't know Doubt before my encounter with Acirema. Sure, unsurety reared its head every supermoon. But true Doubt is a condition. One that leads to faithlessness if given enough room. One rooted in the heart. It slows your tongue and speeds your thoughts. It hears a voice, one it knows to be righteous, and dismisses it in the same breath. One that is equally afraid of success and failure, since they are both unknown. Doubt makes you question the story in your own gut. I would venture to say it is our undoing. It is not often that a god is deceived. Much more frequently, we deceive ourselves of the outcome of fights we are sure we could win.

By the time I made it to middle school, I had already learned how to throw a punch. My father's interim position had transformed into full-time ministry, and my brother took his resentment out on the walls and me. I had learned to be quick in school. I had learned to be quiet at home. My mother, knowing I was smart, sat me down and had a long conversation about how to give time for the dumber kids (though she never called them that) to catch on. This was supposed to keep me out of trouble. She tried to show me how to hold my tongue. The thing about being good with words is it also makes you a threat. I had become a marksman. With

words I could gut you, from heart to mouth, invisible inci-
sion. My mother taught me that too is our burden. By the
time I got to seventh grade, I was more aware than others
how my mouth and body made me dangerous.

I tried to be a good student. I would pick the seat in the
front of the classroom and introduce myself to the teacher
by my full name. Then I would buy time, fighting the itch
in my hand that wanted to jettison out at every question.
I would push my palms flush under my butt. I would shift
side to side and mumble the answer as other kids tried to
show their work. Eventually, after counting down from one
hundred at a snail's pace, I would slowly wave a hand, if no
one had figured it out, and answer. There was so much work
to make myself small.

Group projects were the worst. The natural leader in me
would tire of bickering over the best approach. Leaders with
no backbone infuriated me. And on the rare occasion the
teacher would assign us roles, I ended up picking up the
slack for every procrastinating person in my group. It was
like they didn't understand time. We all had somewhere to
be in life. I had felt the clock ticking since transitioning to
public school. It was time to move. Life around us is always
fleeting, and just because the teacher said we had to spend
three days practicing some skill didn't mean we couldn't get
it faster. I was an insatiable learner, and the teacher always
paired me with struggling students to help get them on task.
Q, Reggie, Ari, Michael—I always got stuck with one of them.

Q was over six feet tall in middle school. A handsome guy with a five-head hairline that he always tried to hide with multicolored do-rags. He was a charmer. Always trying to chase girls when he should've been chasing grades. Reggie was the opposite. Runt of a kid, who was known best for chewing an ink pen until it burst and peeing on himself in the middle of Ms. Johnson's science class. Needless to say, he didn't make the best decisions. Ari was a transfer student who came halfway through the year. He might have held some semblance of intelligence behind his thick Nigerian accent, but he chose to play jester instead. He danced about the classroom with monkey arms and tribal gyrations that reaffirmed every stereotype Americans had about Africans. Then there was Michael. He never struck me as stupid as much as a really slow learner. He was a quiet kid who, by himself, was actually tolerable. He didn't contribute much, which made group work hard, but when he finally got something, he was helpful. I think he was too far into the awkwardness of teenagehood to really care about his grades. He was older, seemed like maybe he had been held back. His face covered in the apocalypse of acne already. He was the kind of guy who went away for summer vacation and came back as the most desirable brown-skin boy in the school. But he was still in his ugly duckling phase. Michael was the perfect base for a chemical reaction, fairly neutral until one of the other boys was added into the mixture. Then all hell broke loose.

In anticipation of Doubt, my mother taught me the Doctrine of the Combat Trinity. I would give myself three chances to question myself before reacting. At each strike of three, I was to examine the rage, make it a promise, and then ask it if its hands were clean. And if they were, I must let it do the things it must. This was also a way to love myself.

That morning, Ms. Pospichal, our favorite history teacher, who somehow lucked into having me and the band of brown boys in the same class, assigned new groups. I got stuck with Michael, Q, and some child I don't remember to work on a map project to create our own island. I guess she figured Ari and Reggie would be enough to control on their own and spared me from the ultimate punishment. After minimal deliberation, our combined love for music led us to create "Stereo Island." Its boom-box-shaped body held all kinds of coves and tundras and deserts, which made it the perfect spectacle of A+ work, or at least that was my plan. Half-way through drawing the shape, Q started kicking Michael under the table and blaming it on me. Then Michael reciprocated by trying to bounce colored pencils off Q's shore (the space before the waves hit). The fury grew in me. I tried to wave down Ms. Pospichal, but her redirection was only temporary.

"Remember what your mother said, three strikes," I mumbled under my breath to rein myself back in. But after just a few moments, Michael was back, this time in my face playing that annoying "I'm not touching you" game. I told him to back up or I would slap him clean into the wall behind him. A promise. Strike one. He laughed it off and inched his body even closer to mine.

"I'm not touching you." His warm breath now close enough to curl my eyelashes.

I stared him down and raised my hand to get Ms. Pospichal's attention, but by now Ari was in full thrash. Ari held her focus, while I flailed wildly, calling out her name.

"I promise you. You need to back up before I slap you." Strike two.

Q began to edge him on.

"Man. She not gonna hit you. You gonna let this girl punk you?"

That was all the reaction Michael needed. He leaned in, his mouth almost touching my eyelids, and whispered, "I'm not touching you." Strike three. My momma didn't raise liars, and I had kept my hands spotless.

The next sound the entire class heard was my hand like the crack a leather belt makes when it slices through the air at the right angle and lands against your skin. I watched Michael in slow motion lift an inch off his seat and plummet into the bulletin board behind him. The entire class turned and watched as a handprint reddened across his cheek. The rest of his face didn't take long to follow suit. Ms. Pospichal ran to our table and asked what happened. He mumbled some sad whimpering mess. Then I told her that he kept messing with me. I told her about the Trinity. I told her I tried to get her attention. I told her he didn't listen. She told me to take my stuff because I "wouldn't be returning." Then she wrote me a referral to the principal's office.

On the long walk down the winding corridor, past the nurse's office, the Acirema's doubtful curse met me again. Showed me how red my hands were. Convinced me that it was my own blood. This self-inflicted wound of the mind. This pain that rings your ears with each blow. And the only way to keep the world from seeing the way I hemorrhaged was to give myself over to the silence. A silence so familiar by then, it might as well be natural.

By eighth grade, I was officially a late bloomer. Ant bites for breasts, but widening hips that filled out skorts that skipped over blacktops on silver-glitter platform sneakers. I spent most of my time outside of my guy group, in the band room. I was a choir nerd. Alto section, who dipped into the tenors when they came up too weak to hold a harmony. Not many my shade, I speckled the back row between some acne-ridden boy child and Amanda. She was soft-faced, with dark hair that made her look more exotic than traditional white. Her long straight bob dangled above her shoulders, and you could hear her smile in every note. She wasn't a sky-praised soprano, but popularity still buzzed around her. I was the youngest by a whole year, since I had skipped a few grades, but I was taller than the entire row, so no one considered me young. That was until the girl chatter spilled like fresh-torn cuts in the wrong direction.

Suddenly everyone was sharing stories about this riverway women go about emerging into womanhood. Your cycle, Momma called it. Though never in the way that meant a healthy ebb and flow, more like a thing that needed to be broken or meant to break you. At home, my cycle meant an all-out inquisition. When I turned thirteen and my panties were bone-dry, it shot up a less-than-red flag in my mother's mind of panic. I went from developing too fast in size to not developing fast enough. This meant visits with specialists to check my hormones, secret conversations every time I emerged from the bathroom, and the constant growing fear that one day, somewhere, ol' Bloody Mary would come for me. I just assumed that's what happened when the girls called for her in the sleepover mirrors. She showed up, stabbed you in the womb, and then you walked around believing you were more woman for it. All of it drove my anxiety through the roof. Holding my breath every time I peed or laughed too hard and something came out. Any moment, it could be upon me, and there was no way to stop it. Now here I was, in this circle of girls bragging about cramps and heating pads, with no blood and no rationale to explain it.

That was when Amanda made me more visible in conversation, asked me directly, said, "Are you on your period right now?"

I shook my head no, trying not to see my mother's worry in her face. Then she leaned closer and said, "Are you sure?" Taking a deep breath. "'Cause I can smell it on you."

I don't know how many parts of me were turning red, but my face was the epicenter. I shook my head harder before running off to the bathroom to confirm I hadn't lied. I sat there thinking how my body must be a failure. After everyone's poking, prodding, and prompting, and still, I was not quite a girl, not quite a woman, doubting if I ever would be more than something reeking from the middle.

The silence leached everything from me. And even once the wombshed came, it led to no vacations from the questioning. No, Doubt just sneaks into your luggage. And every time you believe yourself far enough away to call it respite, it finds a way to stain everything near it.

Keep My Name Out Your Mouth

My first job in Space City landed me as a phone operator for a travel agency. Space City seemed light-years away from my family and the dust-stirring hustle of the City of Angels. It held a much slower pace than even the Empire. Southern drawls sprinkled through their system. Police on horseback. Ten-gallon hats. A strange new frontier. It was humid, and the air was thin. But it offered me a place to hide behind a headset and partial wall that separated the dark-glass room from the real world. Holiday Away promised the freedom of flight for half the price. And while even discounted freedom was out of my price range, sitting this close to it felt like sniffing hope growing in the flower bed of every call. I stealthily waded through the most eclectic mix of people, sending them to agents to plan their trips of a lifetime. From parents planning magical vacations for them and their eleven children, to men trying to disguise their voices to book a trip to Lustopia, a nude island known for its orgy baths and swinging lifestyle. I heard them all. And I had to be the color of quicksand. The unflinching, bland, imperturbable voice they would perceive no differently than the earth. The voice that would suck them into the very thing that gave them flight. The farthest thing from water.

Holiday Away, how may I direct your call?

Uh, yeah, I'm looking for a trip to Poonta Can-Na, Mexico?

[Eyeroll] Are you looking for a resort or a cruise?

Well, I'm not sure. I wanna take one of them there boats up the river? Is that a cruise or a resort?

Please hold while I transfer you to our
cruise department.

I was opaque then. The way Doubt colors you all by
yourself. A voice between importance and reason. A pass-
erby to my own life. Slipping into the purgatory of the call
center, clung to by callers who refused to let go.

Holiday Away, this is the operator. How
may I direct your call?

> Yes, I am wanting to find out what
> kinds of vacations you have to offer?

Are you looking for a resort or a cruise?

> [Screaming:] Honey! Do you think you
> might want a resort or a cruise?
> Well, I don't know, I am asking what
> YOU want!
> The lady asked me and I know you
> get seasick ever since that time with
> Sheila . . .
> No one said anything about Sheila
> going on the trip . . .
> Why do you always have to do this?
> Every time I want to plan a trip, you
> make it so hard.

Sir, can I help direct your call?

> Just a second . . .
> She's trying to ask me a question, and
> I can't hear her.
> Would you stop yelling?!
> Hello?

Yes, ma'am. How can I direct your call?

> Okay, can you tell me more about the
> cruises and resorts, please?

Hold, please.

I cannot say that all I felt was suffering. That is the trick, right? In the thick of it, finding the trick. Every god has a ruse, even if it only helps pass the time. The best calls— and by best I mean most ruse-worthy—were the people who wanted to speak to a manager. Some had legitimate reasons. I remember one traveler who was stuck in a country where tourists were disappearing. This happened when adventurous go-getters left the resort to see the "real" version of the country they were traveling to. Upon paying some local kid to show them around in the impoverished alleys and seedy underbelly they just had to see, they were taken hostage so that the kid could afford to buy his family food. A trick of the natives. If we were lucky, we would be able to connect them to a manager to get them home safely.

Then there was the other kind of manager call. The one of no patience. In this case, the person who had been so irate with their inability to connect or the crushing pressure to purchase for a better price that they had to "speak with a manager." Since each division had only two on duty at a time, we tried to keep the lines as clear as possible for the real emergencies. This equated to longer-than-life wait times for the people who were just sitting at home. This equated to more tests of our ability to turn off any emotions that stirred in us. The passing of the Doubt. Our hope. That the disgruntled customers would get so hopeless in their waiting, they would eventually give up. Since all the operators sat in the same call-center area, we could discuss whose managerial call had the longest wait time and highest priority. For those determined, we could turn time into its own artifice of deceit. This one of the tongue.

I remember the first woman to fall into our trap. Maybe not the first, but one of the most memorable. The age cracked in her voice. I cannot tell you of her initial fury; this I never knew. But from what I could piece together, her service was less than the pristine attention touted in our advertisements.

Holiday Away, how may I—

                    I need to speak with your manager
                    NOW!

Ma'am, may I ask what the concern is
related to so I can get you to the right
manager?

                    [Sigh.] I just need to speak to a
                    manager. Can't you just do that?

Well, in order to get you to the appropriate manager, I have to know a little bit
about your concern.

                    JUST GET ME THE MANAGER!!!!

Hold, please.

And the clock started. We turned the digital hourglass
and continued transferring power between multiple lines.
After a sundial's shift, the original ticking hold time would
pull us back to make sure we hadn't forgotten about anyone in the trick while we were connecting other callers. The
first pull yanked me back, signaling she was still there. Like

a tell-tale heart increasing with madness at each shadow shift.

Ma'am, are you still there?

> Well, where else would I be?
> That's a stupid question.
> You know, you are just like the last
> guy
> who wasn't LISTENING TO WHAT I
> WANTED . . .

Thank you for your patience.

A manager will be with you shortly.

After enough of the sun's shifting, the flickering switchboard would become more violent. Wildly strobing again. Yanking us back to the caller's insistent grip and growing anger, with no intention of letting it slip. She was determined, but there was only a matter of Doubt having enough time to sink its teeth in.

Ma'am?

We are still waiting for the manager . . .

What kind of business is this where
you just put me on hold when I ask to
speak with a—?

Hold please.

Once we were tangled in hold times, a signal could be
wafted up to the manager's table. They would honor the longest hold by lending their ear to whatever ridiculous request
came next. By the time her line flickered me a third time,
by grit or anger, she had outlasted every other complaint. So
when the manager gave the signal to transfer the next call, I
went to retrieve her from her purgatory of waiting. But when
I clicked the line I discovered Doubt had won. Her orneriness
proving no match, she'd hung up. So another call was passed
through. No sooner than it did, one of the other operators
called my name. She said she thought she had my angry cus-
tomer on the line. I laughed. She thought calling back would
give her a better chance of being heard. What silly woman
thinks she can restart her history without acknowledging her
prior shame? Unfortunately, she didn't understand the system. In order to get heard, you had to outlast. You had to wait
your turn, even when your turn seemed unabating. She must
not've experienced Doubt or being under the thumb before to
arrive with such optimism. Her time started over now. I knew
that talking to me was the last thing she wanted. So, in trick's
fashion, I giggled and asked for her to be passed back to me.

Hello, ma'am.

I thought I had lost you.

Is this the manager?

I had a manager for you, but we were
disconnected.

Wait, you're the lady from before . . .

We are currently experiencing a high
volume of manager calls . . .

No, don't put me on hold!

Please hold.

AAAAAAAAAAAAAAAAAAA
AAAAHHHHHHHHHHH!!!!!

Another pass of the sun and she hung up again before
reaching a manager. It always baffled me how far we let
Doubt seep in before we abandon it. I wonder how many
times she questioned the system. Redesigned it in her head.
Knew there was a better way, one more equitable, but had no

ear willing to listen. I too know this plight from her side. For being perceived the weaker of these is only a matter of faulty translation. And what better way for Doubt to sucker punch than to have a way with words?

It brings to mind another caller, equally as memorable. A seasoned woman from the South. Called on a Sunday morning when we were staffed light and my guard was down. Most of the operators were out, so we were tasked to be the human voicemails, typing each message in the system of leads for agents to pull from when they finally clocked in. This helped us keep the phone lines empty but tracked who was responsible for getting back to the callers in a reasonable time. In this system, we could see who retrieved it. The agent couldn't reject the message, because once they opened it, it became their burden. I was working a double with one other operator, when the call came in. Her rasp sat like a gravied biscuit in her throat.

Holiday Away, how may I direct your call?

I wanna find out more about a European river cruise.

Unfortunately, all of our agents in that department are currently handling

other calls. If you would like, I can take
a message and have an agent give you a
call as soon as they become available.

        Okay. That'll be fine.

What is your name?

        Anne.

All right, Ms. Anne, what's your phone
number?

        It's 832——.

I have that message ready to send.
Did you have any special questions or
requests for the agent?

        Well, I have just one.

Yes, ma'am.

        Can you make sure whoever calls me
        isn't one of those Blacks or Mexicans
        or Indians? I need someone who can
        speak English.

This is the part I revisit a thousand times over. I think of an eternity of comebacks, ways to show I could see this coming, but Doubt undoes all weapons. Unloads all guns. Pacifies all needs to be comforted by your own wrath. There was so much I knew I should've said, but only one thing came out.

Noted. You have a wonderful day, ma'am.

You too. God bless.

Then I sat there in the silence. When my coworker asked me what was wrong, I showed her the message. She made the joke, "If that woman only knew who she was talking to . . ." But I hid myself in the wavering so well, even I didn't know who I was.

The Acirema's Doubt may be the greatest colonizer. Takes your tongue first. Your potency next. It will make you lose sight of yourself in your own mirror. The way that the future moves on with such hindsight of the past. Like it would've made better decisions. But Doubt knows how to reach back. Strike a chord that hasn't been heard in centuries in your chest. And if you do not find a way to color over it, you are subject to pity. And no one wants to be pitied. Being pitied is worse than never being believable in the first place. This, a lesson with no short way through.

Sometimes, the most colorful staff in the private school

get away together. Board our own substation. Usually around lunch, when all the prep periods align and our shoulders have held a heavy week of tolerance. This week we took to a small Mexican restaurant close to campus. Just past the fiesta market, after the pupusa stand, just outside the farthest end of the Space City's inner loop. A few blocks from campus. Lupe recommended it. Says it reminds him of the food back home. So Kaitlyn, Myrna, Lupe, and I jump in a white four-door pickup and hit the streets before someone can realize we're missing. Juan follows behind us in his own car; he is headed home early after the meal. We arrive under the red-roofed solace, the smell of fresh tortillas marrying the sizzle of carne asada flautas and chicken fajitas.

The restaurant isn't new, but it isn't quite a hole in the wall. The waitresses wear aprons that look like folklórico dresses, and the buzz of regulars fills the room. The menu has a thousand items, with pictures to boot. And the horchata is made fresh near the entrance. A telenovela plays on the small TV that sits catty-corner to our table. The volume is down. I watch as they mouth truths and deceptions, their cold shoulders thawing into forbidden embraces. We can't hear a word, but every message is clear.

We sit at a square table near the center of the room, and each of us grabs a menu, all but Lupe, who always seems to know what he wants . . . in everything. Juan joins us. And the unloading begins. A priest asked during the diversity training if we were going to have "Mexican snacks." He then listed these as "Takis and Dos Equis." Pass. A priest decided to use an anecdote in his sermon that required a bad Jamaican accent to portray a native Belizean man . . . for thirty-five minutes. Pass. My white Teacher Leader told me not to worry, because he didn't plan on treating me like "an overseer" the entire year. Pass. Then Kaitlyn says it. "At least none of you have to hear about Bertha." The shoulders around the table roll, eyes find the ceiling, the floor. The whole group is a heavy sigh except me.

"Bertha?"

It is here where the group brightens to a vibrant blush. I am an obvious outlier, uninformed enough to make the shift. They are a sea of red faces realizing all my unknowing, all my innocence they will have to take.

"You don't know about Bertha," she says shamefully. "You know Margaret?" The redhead with the distended jaw and the awkward smile? The one who brags about her raisin potato salad? Well, "she has a ninety-one-year-old Black woman who works for her family. She was passed down through the years. She says she helped raise her father."

"The father that just passed away?"

"Yes."

"The judge?"

"Yes."

"The one that lived in bumfuck Bootville?"

A neighboring planet.

"She said she is her best friend. Posts pictures of her on Instagram."

"Does she get paid?"

"I don't know."

"So she has a . . ."

"She bragged once about how the family gave her a car. Says she should be grateful that they keep her so well outfitted."

Juan, practical Juan, sits watching me, ready for a pragmatic response about naivety and how racism isn't always blatant but sometimes stems from years of ignorance. This time he is a dramatic monologue in pantomime. All I hear is my heartbeat, like feet running through the backwoods of the South in the middle of the night: rebellious. I feel the blue coursing faster through my veins. My hands tighten and my stomach knots. My plate is empty, but I want to give it back. Lupe is angered again by Bertha's name. I ask, who all knows?

"Everybody. I'm surprised you haven't heard her talk about her before."

Margaret doesn't talk to me. Barely makes eye contact. And it all makes sense.

The table begins to joke about creating shirts that say "Free Bertha" and wearing them to school one day. The cacophony of laughter encases me again. The chips and salsa are refilled. The conversation moves on. Pass. Pass. Pass. I am stuck still choking on her name, trying to find the shortest route to Bootville on the maps app, questioning how it has been so long and we are still in the same scene.

And this is the part when the Doubt creeps into you. Is it Time you seek as your scapegoat? To say this must've been any moment outside of the one you breathe is a cop-out. Is it Reaction you seek to justify? Would you have flipped the tables? Made a protest sign? Started a riot? Who is to say that I didn't want the same things in my own way. Have you considered the damage that words can render? I used all my angst to pen a poem for her that read in part:

> *She speaks of her the way one*
> *speaks of machines, How their*
> *gears rust*
>
> *a vintage find*
> *91 years in still finding a way to work*

I left it for them. I know that is not the activism you wanted, but Kaitlyn liked it. Says it gave her chills. Asks if she can share it with Abby. Then, that afternoon, Ryler comes to me. Says the poem was "moving." I don't know who gave it to him. I hope they give it to Margaret. That it festers. Viral. Fear's ivy spreading through her lungs.

But I can't stop thinking about her. Bertha. She sits on my chest the way green thickets into lost. I have looked for her for hours. Yesterday, I found her in a private post next to an ever-smiling Margaret. A dozen smiles around a birth-day cake. And then there is cold-faced Bertha. Sparkless eyes. Jaw clenched as Margaret tightens her hand around a frail arm. Picture after picture fill Margaret's feed. Effervescent captors over Bertha's sullen sulk.

My gut makes me look for Bertha's address online. I already have a friend with a fast car who is willing to drive straight through the darkness of Bootville. I stumble across Margaret's father's obituary. I scan for any sign of bravado, any open boast of all that he has conquered. Then I see it. At the end of a long list of sisters-in-law, half brothers, grandnieces. There it is: "survived by a longtime family friend, Bertha." As if to say they will never be through with her.

It would be easy here to walk away. I know how challenging this all may be for you. But what an exercise in faith to believe this may be the truth of it. That I still find myself at the bottom of Doubt's boot. That I always have been. I have envisioned a double-blind life more times over than I can count. I have revisited those trees. I have looked into that moon. I have wondered what would happen if I made it all go away again. Wondered why she didn't.

If I returned to someone's property I
would poison my self-serving
owner's food.

Couldn't leave no witnesses.
Would have to punish the lot,
Be my own
witch doctor and summon the shakes.

Watch the table convulse levitate
off their seizing knees.
The jeering of loosened shackles
A jubilant tambourine

I have never considered
It being a padlocked heart.
One so heavy it stays
for seventy-five years just to know

that someone knows your name.
though it may only be to fetch a plate
To make them so full they burst

But I am not my own monolith. And doubting that there is strength, still there, even when we cannot see it, is losing the explosion in the length of the fuse. No, fire burns in different colors. A Black body absorbs all frequencies. But do not forget that it knows how and when to emit them too.

Badass Bertha. I bet you she has a fist tattooed on her left breast and a barrel on her right. That she often leaves the soap out of their laundry and laces their lemonade with bleach. And they sit on the porch together, on the swing that thinks it sees everything, sipping the end like it was sweetened with black agave. I bet you there is where her smile hides itself and waits for the right moment. That she is buying time in every one of Margaret's Instagram posts of her clipping her toenails or shouldering the load. That she whispered her manumission in their final moments. She is the puppet master extraordinaire. She has tricked Time into thinking it can hold her back, only to wrestle its mighty thumb to the grave and still inherit it all to pass on. And how dare I interrupt that.

Though it may always live inside us, we do not have to make this apprehension our master. I have learned this one thing to be true. There is only one way to cure the disease of Doubt. You must fight it out.

So I returned to my youth, around sixth grade, when my mother gave me and my brother an ultimatum. Stay in home-school or venture out into a new field and see if we could grow in public school. I was content here with my once-a-week interactions with our community group for "park day" and my self-driven plot of learning, but my brother wanted more. He was going into high school and he wanted the typical high school experience: the girls, going to prom, the girls, going to football games on Friday nights, the girls ... But my mother told us it was all or nothing; either everybody leaves or everyone stays. So my brother, in the same way he convinced me to give him all my Lego one week after getting them for Christmas, had a talk with me over the summer. By fall, we were both entering public school.

By now, we had lost the house and were living in the Township of Dust. It was up the hill from where the freeway interchanged to drive deeper into the City of Angels or head farther up the coast. Not quite distant enough to be the Empire and not quite ceremonious enough to be the City; it was limbo. A dusty passing ground with a dinosaur park in the distance. It was most known for the mountain that someone built a giant letter *C* on the side of with large white stones that could be seen from the nearby highway. I always wondered what it stood for. *Captive?*

About a mile up the road sat Sunshine Elementary School. The concrete campus was built on a series of man-made plateaus, so the row of temporary buildings could sit just above the playground and cafeteria. I don't remember seeing color before Sunshine. My mom says that she and my father intentionally bought their last house with the United Nations for neighbors. All the various shades of kids played freely together so well that we never stopped to compare skin. But near Sunshine, there was only one student who baked in the afternoon sun as long as me. Her name was Shacola, like Sha-Cola. As you can imagine, she was made fun of every day. They called her "Shasta cola" and asked her if they could drink, spill, or pour her out. I knew how she felt. They targeted me for all kinds of reasons: my legs sprouted faster than the rest of my body, my hair was a rubber-band ball of frizz, not to mention I tried to be quiet but fell short out of utter boredom most days. They would speak around us in a Spanish so thick and exaggerated it *had* to be about us. Or those with no accent would point and laugh themselves into tears. Shacola and I clung to each other for pure survival. I tried to look out for her.

Until the day her mother withdrew her.

I have my suspicions of what straw broke her. But no matter, she was gracious enough to leave all the light shining on me. Like the clouds parted and the gods recommended my name to the ensuing vines. They came for me like an all-consuming thrush. In class, they would cough insults under their breath every time I raised my hand to answer, which was often. Coming from homeschool, I was bored. I was so tired of students taking days to grasp what I understood to mastery in hours.

Recess was the worst. I would play tetherball, and they would surround me screaming and yelling to throw me off my game. I felt like I was being smothered. Like they were weaving a mat above me and planned to hold it down over my mouth until I could no longer breathe. But even weeds bloom a bud to try to convince you they belong.

Across the room, Little Miss Flowers burst forth, lily pale and just as delicate. She was one of a handful of poor white students who found their way into this school. Despite her family's poverty, she still carried so much privilege, like a hummingbird chose her first, and as soon as her petals truly opened she would be rid of us. She sat with her back to me and always seemed to be focused on her work. We rarely had any interaction, until the day she asked me to play her in handball at recess. No one ever seemed to notice me enough to invite me to anything. I was excited just to avoid my daily rumbles behind the trees that lined the blacktop.

It was like tradition, at recess, a group of kids would line up at the base of the blacktop where the white line marked the foul line. Before us stood a large wooden wall perfect for taking and receiving the pummeling of that red rubber ball. I flourished here. It was me versus the wall, and very little mattered. I had already weeded out dozens of other students who tried to step into my garden, but she dared to challenge me? I was excited to show her who belonged here and who didn't. I let her serve out of pity, knowing this would be over soon after it started. I thwacked my fist into the ball and launched it back against the grain. Little Miss Flowers lobbed it high above the midway point, serving me the perfect bounce. I returned it with a steady thrust. She almost tripped running behind me to catch it high and knock it down. I laughed at how hard she was working. I cocked my hand back and shattered the earth with a large thwack. She was out of breath and barely reached the return. It dribbled off her hand, bounced once before hitting just above the line at the base of the wall and dribbling twice before I could touch it. Out. I'm out? In my own yard? I stood staring at the wooden planks as they echoed the crowd's jeers. Just then I heard Little Miss Flowers, thorns and all, say, "Get off the court, you little nigger girl!"

I do not doubt it. Instead, I light the fuse.

When I came to, her neck was between my hands. I was vehemently shaking her like a bouquet of love-me-nots. Her face was darkening to violet, and her hair was the descension of deceitful petals. I shook until life all but loosed her. I heard myself—*Are you planning on killing her?* And in a gasp I considered what kind of hand I shall rule with. I dropped her to the ground. The crowd that had gathered around us to watch me throw the bouquet no longer wanted to catch my hands. I stepped over her debris and made my way back to the classroom. And the bell rang.

A scar tells a story of the day
life got too close and you had to
put it in its place.

A Lie Don't Care Who Tells It

I would like to tell you that my present is an extension of that culminating moment. Maybe there is a universe where it is. Where everyone learned that there is a line, and fury on the other side of it. But even when fighting for yourself, in this skin, there is almost always a consequence.

I sat in class for ten minutes before they called me to the office. Little Miss Flowers, of course, went and told the principal that I tried to turn her to potpourri on the blacktop. I was indifferent. I knew what I had done and I was proud of it. I packed up my belongings and headed for the principal's office.

I entered that sterile box that held the principal's out-of-scale, larger-than-life desk that was flanked in front by two smaller chairs—sitting just far enough apart to stop another scuffle. Behind him, Acirema's flag hanging limp and at ease.

Little Miss Flowers sat there, red-hot. Her face was still recovering its standard blood flow. I sat in the empty chair, across from her and the principal, cocked my head to the side, and folded my arms across my chest. Then he began the inquisition:

"She says something happened at lunch—is that true?"

"Yes, sir."

"Would you like to tell me what happened?"

"She called me a nigger, so I choked her."

"You admit that you assaulted Miss Flowers."

"She called me a nigger."

Then here she comes, chiming in, like anybody asked her anything:

"She tried to kill me and then called me a bitch!"

Had I been so out of my body that my tongue did its own dance? *Bitch?* Not a word I craved the flavor of. No, my mother said women don't use that word. It is made for rabid beasts. And wasn't I becoming a woman? Weren't we both? My mother didn't raise any liars. And I wasn't going to carry a burden I didn't deserve.

"I didn't say that! She called me a nigger and then I shut her up."

The principal rolled his eyes. Then the punishment. The "keep your hands to yourself" talk, the "it's not okay to touch someone else's body" stuff. It's funny, in all of that, he never once said, "It isn't okay to use the word *nigger*," but *bitch* was a sword sharpened in Hell's flames.

It's something to know that your Black shrouds your Woman. That your strength can be cut down at a single accusation. Maybe this is where I first doubted the Pink Approach. This movement that exalts form over color. This suffrage that pushes us to suffer at the back of the progress line. That office became high grass where my body split in two, too far away from itself to reach its own agreements. Forever in war for which is more important, on a pedestal made for one. Even midchoke, Miss Flowers was thinking of a way to paint her mouth an excusable offender, to bloom another day. But what to do with all this woman I wasn't anymore? This rite of passage no body should earn?

Some gods would tell you that this is why you must work twice as hard to get half as much. But I know that half is not the holy grail. Tell a half-full belly that it is satisfied and see how it grumbles. I did not come from the wombs of half-baked women bartering for crumbs from Artemis's table. No, I come from venomous side-eyes that could strike your heart cold halfway across a room with only a single look.

The way Momma tells it:

Ma'Dea used to spend the day cleaning the houses of white women to make ends meet. Said she would take her along for the ride sometimes. They would walk into some big fancy house where the floors that used to be worked by southern property sat dull, awaiting their hands and knees that found their way to freedom. It was hard work. She would take all the pennies she earned and store them up for a big meal, like a Thanksgiving Day feast. Ma'Dea would spend all day making the fixin's: macaroni and cheese, greens, turkey, ham, mashed potatoes, hot-water cornbread . . . Make your jaw unlatch just thinking 'bout it.

This year was like all the rest. After months of hard work, their hungry bellies accordioned a praise to the coming of a holiday supper. They slid into the neighborhood market, like always, to get all the stuff that didn't grow in the garden out back. Must've spent all the money Ma'Dea had scrubbed out of the floors in one trip. She spared no expense topping off the paper bags. But before they could get out the door, the white woman behind the counter accused Ma'Dea of padding the bags with things she didn't buy. Tried to make a whole scene like she was a charmer or something.

Ma'Dea looked down at my mother, wrestled the truth against her dormant fangs, slithered back to that checkout counter ready to strike. Then remembered how easy it is to cut the head off when you have a mob privileged to carry shovels. She cast the groceries off like shedding skin, all over the counter. Constricted around my mother's empty belly till it felt full, hissed for her money back.

She swallowed her pride whole that day, like it was a person trapped inside her just wanting not to be the meal.

She knew that every fight is not made in our image. Every protest, not our sign.

My mother used to tell me that women's voices weren't measured on a balanced scale. That we had to overcome the mass of our darkness. That talking loud only worked if you were saying something worth hearing. And when it came to the Pink Approach, my mother made sure my ears were wide open.

Do you know how much bras cost? I had to work too hard to afford more than one in the first place. Don't you like a roof over your head? A full plate? I can't take off to strike. Won't be a job to come back to. Don't you know we only boycotted *on* our commute? We haven't ever stopped, maybe slowed down. What's more frustrating than not grinding? Grinding at a snail's pace, *with* your bra on. What I look like burning money? Burning hard work. So I could have the right to slave and make less. *And* my chest hurts. *And* my clothes don't fit right. Weren't my babies hungry enough? My back grieved enough? Don't I deserve support? All this flesh bouncing free. You gonna tell me I don't need armor for a battle that wasn't ours in the first place. And is anybody striking for us?

She knew already that knowing when to attack is just as important as being able to. This is true in war and love. There is no liberation for us in being the distressed damsel. No poignant end to lingering with dragons. Dragons have their own incentive. There is no one coming to save us here.

We must hope for a palace. One that is made in the in-betweens. Where we can be both shadow and ball gown, both charred and our own fueling fire. This is why we love so recklessly. For what is love but a risk to be seen and not feared?

And then there was Good. Somebody said his name once. Thurgood, maybe. Something formal and way too proper to fit all of his bad boy. Good was Nubian, with a smile as wide as the panhandle, though he wasn't from Space City, or anywhere in the State of Lonely Stars for that matter. He had that midwestern swagger that reeked of the City of Motors or the City of Winds. Somewhere only found by the Great Migration. Somewhere near a factory or an automotive plant. And he . . . he was the gasoline. Took flight sometime after high school.

We would spark into each other at random poetry events, art shows, and the like. He would always find a way to slide his chest up against my back in the manner that made everybody in the room feel safer. But we weren't together or anything. Just a craving. Like when summer hits and someone dangles the thought of ice water and your mouth dries up even more.

Good was a flirt. The charismatic type. Simultaneously one of those Hoteps who believes in conspiracy theories, denies Christ's existence, wears Black Power T-shirts, buys incense from the local Reggae Bodega on Almeda, but uses the word *nigga* like it's all-consuming. He was born in the wrong era. Woulda been a Huey or a Fred. Woulda loved the Angela in me. Praised the Black woman's body. Told me what he would do to it, in jest. Or promise. But he wasn't really interested.

Just wanted to hang, city's center, at Beaucoup Wings N Wings for the open-mic night. Wallflower with commentary on every piece. I think I saw him touch the mic once. He laughed through the entire two minutes, but nobody minded. That smile. He would sit next to me and lean his shoulder into mine. Lick his lips then bite. Damn. Butterfly-ass Black man. The kind that's beautiful to watch but can't touch without it killing something. He would joke about the size of my hair and hips and then linger too long around the punch line. I would want to sucker punch him right in the lips with my heart. But we weren't ever gonna be more than mouse and wildcat over two bottles of house-crafted lemonade that made your lips pucker and your eyes roll back. I came to regret all the space that stretched between us.

Until that night. We had all joked about a Black president for years, but for the last few months it was a rising possibility. We watched Barack Obama gaining traction. He was our woke, spades, shit-talking point. Half of us were sure his success would end in assassination, and the other half never thought he would get elected in the first place. But somehow here we were, back at Beaucoup's, watching a map of the country slowly blueing, state by state. Good arrived after I had already taken my place near the bar.

Beacoup's was more packed than I had ever seen, though the streets outside were quiet for a college neighborhood. He pressed his chest to my back but refused to look me in the eye. Then, he smiled and loudly announced, "This nigga bout to win the presidency," in the proudest voice he could muster. The crowd was abuzz, all waiting for the largest states with the most power to change from a dull gray to a vibrant cobalt. The shit-talking filled the moments between. Whether news predictions or commentary on how the country was changing, the hope was palpable.

That wasn't the moment I planned on admitting that I didn't vote for Barack the first time around. And no, I didn't vote for *him* either. The same year, the Green Party had a Black woman with a Latina running mate on their ticket. Both women were wildly charismatic. I had the opportunity to weave a poem for their rally that summer. I agreed with almost every point of their platform, aside from the abolition of the prison system entirely. That seemed slightly unattainable. However, their pros outweighed the ambiguous hope speech of Obama. While I wanted to back a Black president, was it too much to ask for a woman? The young hopeful in me just knew that she could buck the system. To be the first Black anything, you have to have lizard skin. Must be able to see the daggers coming from your own jungle. Must be willing to become an exhibit in scrutiny in a habitat not your own. Willing to be held to a standard no one else knows exists. And doesn't that sound like us? There is an activism in just holding space. And the first Black president had to do so flawlessly.

I now know that this world must want to listen to change. But there, standing with Good, neither of us knew what we were asking for. We just knew that our bodies were warm and alive and visible. Then the roar. The announcement that history had to reckon with us. Good turned to me, without warning dipped me back, and pressed his soft warm lips to mine. I wanted to hold on longer, but before I could revel, he was halfway across the bar jumping up and down screaming with joy. I was flush and full. I remember thinking, if Barack Obama made this happen, then "Yes we can!"

When we poured out from the bar, Good was nowhere to be found. The streets were lined with police. Their lights were flashing, and bullhorns announced that a curfew was being put in place. They expected a riot. The way they do at any breeze of us feeling something. But we just quietly went back to our cars, too full of all the fire building in our lungs for all that was now possible.

See? Even loving us is a political act. One we entangle deeply with hope. But Hope may be the scariest thing we grow. Hope of being loved. Hope of having dominion. Of even being on equal ground. Of being held. Of being something unrecognizable to ourselves for a chance at a better outcome.

When I was eight, I once tried peeing like a man. Wanted

to wield all that power between my lifelines. Wanted to be able to stand and let the care fall from me. I faced the toilet, straddling legs around the mouth of the porcelain beast. Readied myself to aim, to manumit all the impotence, the golden secrecy. To show my body knows how to shoot straight too. I fought the urge to squat into familiar submission. Be the woman I was trained to be. But liberation is not a controlled stream. Before I could stop it, I was everywhere. Embarrassingly empty. Feeling less like I owned a new power and more like I abandoned my throne.

The truth may be that we can be nothing more than what we are. That we must hope that this world around us will come to accept what it may not understand. That it will start to believe in us the way we believe in it. And though I have searched Time seven times over and found that Progress never masters longevity, at least for us, that shouldn't stop us from sowing Hope.

The night of *his* election, I fell asleep. I had spent the entire day listening to the what-ifs from my progressive, liberal, White coworkers. Most of their rainbow flags trembling at the fear that he would repeal gay marriage. And while that was a real threat with the recent laws, there were so many additional reasons I feared him becoming president: his previous support of the three-strikes rule, his villainizing Black bodies, his financial support of gentrification. I was tired of watching over all the horrendous outcomes.

But that leaf-falling night, I felt like there was no winning. So I went to bed right after singing sleep over my daughter. By morning, the chirp of birds met hollow wind and the feeling that the deed had been done. I rolled over, picked up my phone, and opened my browser to the news that *he* had won. My first instinct was to divert to an alternate timeline. But in every one I found great progress only met with bigger thumbs. If history had its way, this soil would tell of Michelle in mourning clothes, but enough of us pushed back. I remember rising to disappointment but not disbelief. Bertha's spirit stirring. I knew I had to get back to work.

A new job had pulled me across town two years earlier. One side of the bull's-eye to the other. I thought abandoning my formal teaching job for something more community centered would make room for greater impact. I landed at a literary arts organization positioned in the affluent Museum District that worked at "giving back" to students all over the Space City. This time, my boss was a woman. In fact, most of the office was filled with women. And while only one other shared my hue, I was tired of being talked down to by the older men who felt I had nothing wise to offer. This was meant to be my fresh start, a place where I would relish arriving at the office early. The introvert in me has always loved the quiet moments. I could spend all morning making calls and sending emails in my solitude and then disappear to do campus visits and work with students to sharpen their tongues in the afternoon, returning to quick chats over hummus in the communal kitchen or recommendations of woman-centered grants that just became available. But that morning's arrival came with an unexpected twist.

In the place of merriment and hope that existed just twenty-four hours before sat a chill that only comes with shattered delusion. I wrapped myself in the maroon sweater I kept over the back of my chair for the days the other women had hot flashes. The first couple employees arrived, two white women dressed from head to toe in smudged cinder. Like the whole world had burned down. Then the next few, also all dressed in ash. By the time the office was full, I was clearly the red dress at the funeral. One of the Women in Soot came and sat on the chair near my desk in disbelief. Her eyes filled with water, and she lamented about how disappointed she was with this country. She told me all about how she felt knowing that she wasn't safe, said she couldn't imagine living every day in this fear. I couldn't help but crave popcorn.

When she was done, Monie, the only other one with skin like mine in our office, arrived in a rainbow of clothing. She felt the chill and nodded to ask me what was up, in the way we do without words. Did I mention this sight gave us that too? I replied, "Trump." We laughed.

Our boss came in and sat on a chair in our office. Pink gleaming from behind her black collared shirt. She took a pensive breath and began to explain how she never personally felt this targeted before. She just knew he would undo all the progress they had made. She began to well up. She and her wife feared how their lives may change. She worried that the public beatings and suicides among young queer teens would continue to rise. Monie and I watched as the black she wore felt more like skin. There was part of me that wanted to empathize. If no one understood what it felt to wait for Fear at your back door, it was me. To wonder if the thing you couldn't change would be the thing to herald Death's name. Monie had an extra layer, with her love for men and women. Some days I worried for her even more, but we had lived as Fear's neighbor for so long. And this election was nothing more than a familiar smell from a bordering yard. But the Women in Soot had never lived here before, on this street where you wonder whether your children will return home unboxed and breathing. Whether you will either. Seen when they just wanted to blend in with safety. And so many had never considered that there was a reality outside their own that had always lived nearby. One that was native and homegrown. Fear unbridled.

When she left our office to join the wake at the water cooler, Monie and I couldn't help bursting into laughter. It wasn't a malicious pointed finger. I imagine it was the laughter my great-great-grandmother passed down when the slave master hurt himself whipping our mothers too wildly. This laughter said, "Now you get it, you understand. The work can really begin."

Is this not the thing that brings you and me here? The work? This need for you to comprehend? To measure the lengths we have gone through to make this land a home? For all of us? What we have endured to prove that we belong here? The trick to surviving? You still have no faith that we have seen enough suffering to warrant reverence? Then there must be more convincing left to do. Maybe I need to stir a movement. It is the way of this land. Maybe a march, like the pink tide that was organized in response to the grieving.

The Women in Soot throughout the land were outraged that this country could do what it has always found a way to do. They set out to make the streets bleed pink. Dawned fuzzy labia hats and drew their pickets with heavy markers. If it sounds like I am jaded toward this approach, I cannot say you are wrong. While they garner much attention, marches offer equal access to violence and apathy. Whether tear gas baths or Million Man stands that promise "or else" with no clearly defined retaliation, goers often leave feeling they have accomplished something by treading ground. A feeling fleeting and forgettable. A picture taken of bodies stretched out on Congress's steps. I have seen enough bodies in my days.

But the Women in Soot, the ones who grieved over the copier, they were a new kind of ecstatic when they heard of a national march on the horizon. They started buying T-shirts and requested the day off in such mass that we discussed closing the office early. But I just felt disconnected. Is there nothing to say of solidarity, you ask? Wasn't I still a woman?

Women like me were quickly reminded that all marches are not created equal.

For every Woman in Soot marching, there were five of us on the sidelines. An outcry, one so muffled you could almost ignore it, an independent rising. This march wasn't for us. Never consulted us. Pushed the voices of Black Women in leadership out. Said that listening would be too political. As if a march isn't an act of politics. Just consult the pictures. A handful of community weavers, who sacrificed their greatest concerns for their visibility, in a sea of pink. They just forgot us. City by city. Coast by coast. This thing, this Pink Approach, has a tendency to be so zealous that it runs us over without a second thought. Our womanness should unite us, but it only gives a certain level of equilibrium. Whether or not you have found faith, to be the darker sister is to rub the feet of the liberated female worker, without ever questioning when you clock out.

A separate thought began to splinter off. *We* began to give in to the song of our own march, one that didn't continue to discount the laws stacked against us. We began to organize for the spring, but this time, it was less about *him*. This was about the master choosing an ebony mistress over the monogamy of the house. This was about how the right to weigh in left out complicated skin. This was about Sarah Baartman and Rosie the Riveter, who mocked her outside her cage. This time, we aimed directly at the Pink.

I didn't try to explain the initial march to my daughter, though it may have been one of the first historic things she was alive to witness. Instead, I logged online and added matching shirts for her and me to my cart. Royal blue with an afro-donning woman in the center, sporting large gold hoop earrings, inscribed "Melanin Magic." Then I grabbed a couple children's books on protests and marches that I could share with her. I readied us for *our* march. My daughter fell in love with the mothers before us: Ruby Bridges and Rosa Parks. She dreamed of Audrey Faye Hendricks and craved to know more. She was fairly woke for four. We laid out our ironed pride and jeans and readied ourselves for the march made for us.

The day still had the brisk of a longed-for spring in the air. When we arrived, Emancipation Park was fairly empty. I knew we had been a little early. We grabbed donuts at our favorite small bakery, and I let her run some of the sugar off at the playground. After about an hour, we heard that they were holding a meeting for the ally volunteers across the street at the historic Eldorado Ballroom. That was also the closest open bathroom, and the morning orange juice was becoming too much for the dancing child's bladder. I grabbed her hand from the merry-go-round and pulled her across Elgin Street.

Ascending the stairs, we saw that the ballroom was full of men and women, predominately white, who'd come to help with the march. We ducked into the small restroom, washed our hands, and emerged just as the leaders for the day were taking the stage. The training was held by a charming woman like us and her compassionate white counterpart. They stood in the center of the room, at first waiting for the volunteers to settle in. The white woman welcomed the crowd, told them how important it was they were there. She then introduced the Black woman and gave the floor completely to her. The spirit of a true ally is the fine line between taking the space of someone else's voice and knowing when to set the stage and step aside. While she was only there for a moment, her presence justified. It heralded and validated every word her co-presenter followed with for those not sure who or what to believe. I was inspired. We watched for a minute before my daughter pulled at my arm and begged to return to the swings.

By the time we headed back, the hill beneath the pavilion was full. There were women holding recycled yard signs that they were painting into protest signs, artists, vendors, and women of every shade, size, and age. My daughter jumped straight into painting until she created a sign she was proud of, holding it at arm's length to show me. As she did, the volunteers marched over en masse, all sporting their black "Trust Black Women" shirts. My daughter, perplexed, looked up and pulled the hem of my jacket.

"Yes, sweetheart?"

"Mommy, their shirts say 'Trust Black Women.' Is that because we don't trust white women?"

I ran through every possible answer, knowing this would be a defining moment. Should I tell of how dangerous Pink ideas are? Point out how they have always left us in the blind spot? Jade her for life? I ran through the list of women who had hurt me, then I remembered Mary. Cindy. Two women who helped raise me. Who each boasted of their Black children in front of gawking white eyes. I never doubted either truly loved us like her own. Then there was Donna, my Sunday school teacher who welcomed me to her table, time after time. Meggie, Hannah, Emilie, Kate, my co-conspirators, and a sea of other White women who realized that their shining didn't involve dimming our lights. All of them Pink in some way.

I leaned down and said, "Babe, that's not what they mean. Some people don't trust women made like us. Those shirts are just reminding them that there's a reason they should."

That night, when I tucked her in for bed, her question echoed through my head. So I tucked her in tight, said a prayer, and told her the story of Enilder.

What Happens in This House Stays

There were once two queendoms that straddled two sides of Enilder's glorious mountain. One side was completely illuminated by light, while the other was cooled by the never-ending shade. When Enilder, the god of division, was handing out parcels, he gave the side full of sun to those with the most melanin and the side full of shade to those with the least.

On the light side, the sun beat hot against the earth. While there was no shade given, the bronze villagers worked together, day in and day out, to erect structures to protect their crops from scorching. They knew each other by name and celebrated with every piece built. The water mines gave the people just enough water not to die of dehydration while building their next shelter. Their queen, Queen Ebon, spent her time bathing under Ra's kiss. She lay beneath the first arches erected by the people, drinking hibiscus and rose water mined by their hands. For her, every day was like summer, and her subjects loved her.

On the shade side, every day was like the solace of winter. The pale villagers recoiled into their homes. The brisk shade provided as little warmth as it did light. They busied themselves indoors and rarely spent any time together. They built picket fences of bone to keep out unwanted guests. Since few plants can survive in such little sun, the shade-dwellers became dependent on food baskets that were delivered every day from the other side of the mountain. The queen of the shade, Queen Karen, was a beautiful ice queen who ruled with a scepter of tears. Whenever the deliveries were late or her villagers wouldn't listen, she would push the scepter out in front of her, and great tears of snow would begin to tumble from Enilder's face like an avalanche. Each time, the tears would kill the couriers, and the villagers would have to take months to dig themselves out of the dunes of white tears that piled into mounds and froze them into their homes. The shade-dwellers learned early to keep Queen Karen happy and the food on time, but they feared what she would do at any moment.

While they were rich in crops, the light-dwellers constantly bickered over water. Queen Ebon put strict laws in place to ration the water, but no matter how well she laid out the plans, her subjects always found a way to want more. She tired of the people ignoring her best-articulated plans for their greed of longer baths. So she called the Wise Sisters to come up with a new way to motivate the people to take more responsibility, but this only caused more bickering. Then one day, the couriers were returning from a delivery and passing through the halls of the palace. The Wise Sisters overheard a few couriers talking about one of Queen Karen's avalanches. They spoke of destruction and devastation, but all the Wise Sisters heard was opportunity. If they could get ahold of Queen Karen's scepter, they could cause it to snow on the light side. The sun would melt all the frost into water and all Queen Ebon's people would have an endless supply to fill the bathing pools for daytime parties.

The Wise Sisters ran to meet Queen Ebon to suggest a new plan. One adviser suggested making offerings to Enilder to divide his people into civil war so Queen Karen would hand over the scepter, but Queen Ebon saw no need to cause any war with the neighboring lands. Another suggested offering five hundred cowries as a gift for the staff, but Queen Karen wasn't just going to give up her power, and besides, those on the light side didn't need more, they just needed to ration what they had. Before long the bickering led to so much contention that the Wise Sisters abandoned the plan in front of Queen Ebon. But behind her back, they were summoning the couriers.

The Wise Sisters told the couriers to meet them at a secret cave near the base of Enilder's mountain. They told them to take an extra palette of food with them this time.

The extra palette would require extra hands. Then, while Queen Karen was trying to figure out where to place all the extra produce, the additional courier could sneak into her palace and steal the scepter of tears. They were instructed to hide it in one of their baskets and bring it straight to the Wise Sisters. They must tell no one about the plan, lest they be outcast to the shade side for good. They agreed.

The next day, the couriers set out to deliver the baskets of food to the shade side of Enilder's mountain. They took an extra palette and extra hands, just like the Wise Sisters requested. In trying to manage all the extra food, Queen Karen laid down her staff and gave the perfect opportunity for the courier to snatch it and tuck it into his basket.

But one of the couriers couldn't shake his nerves.

When Queen Karen began to question him about the extra food, he quickly tried to spin the conversation, but he just began spiraling. He asked her for extra money and stirred the palace into such a ruckus that she grew strong with anger and called for someone to bring her the scepter to put an end to this. When her servant reported it was missing, she kicked everyone out and sent for a village-wide search of her precious staff.

The couriers were happy they had gotten away with such a brilliant feat, but they feared what would happen if Queen Karen realized they were the thieves. They returned to the meeting place in a hurry and delivered the staff to the Wise Sisters. They held the crystal staff, passing it between them in awe. They looked through it, adoring each granular stalactite converging within. The Wise Sisters knew, in order to have the greatest effect, they would need to get to the highest point in the land. They would need to get into Queen Ebon's palace.

They waited until Queen Ebon laid out in the sun for her daily basking. Then the Wise Sisters snuck in the front door, crept up the grand staircase, and headed for her bedroom. The day was full of swelter, and the large bay window could see far and wide across the light side of the mountain. They weren't sure how to use the scepter. Then one of the Wise Sisters remembered that she'd heard that Queen Karen held it out in front of her and waited for a response from Enilder. Queen Ebon must've heard their discussion, because just as they were extending their arms, she caught them on her balcony. Queen Ebon was furious. She stormed over, snatching the scepter and accidently thrusting it out, away from their hands. Before she could realize what she had done, the snow had begun to fall.

Queen Ebon stood on the balcony overlooking the makeshift roofs and scorched outer ring. She watched as the frost melted and people rejoiced, holding out buckets and cupped hands to revel in the newly fallen rain. She wondered if maybe she had made a mistake, maybe this plan was meant to give the people things she only dreamed she could give. Then, in the distance, she saw something approaching. First, it looked like ants crawling on the horizon, but before long, the spears of bone began to tell a different story. Queen Karen and her army were coming to regain the scepter.

By now, large waves of white began to descend from the mountain, melting into a cascading waterfall as the water neared the light side of the mountain. Queen Karen didn't know what to do. Sure now what had become of her scepter, she grew even more furious. She commanded her troops to storm the castle. They breached the entrance and headed for Queen Ebon's quarters. But Queen Ebon had her own troubles to tend to.

She had accidently commanded Enilder's tears, but the staff wasn't made for her. What had come quickly refused to retreat. Though she pulled the staff into her chest time and time again, Enilder's tears wouldn't cease. She yelled at the Wise Sisters so loudly that they fled down to the land in fear. The waters continued to rise, washing out the roofs newly built and ones there since the beginning of time. The arches bent under the weight of the tide. The villagers began abandoning buckets for pieces of sparse wood. Anything that would keep them from going under. Queen Ebon watched as many of them weren't strong enough. Villager after villager disappearing beneath the crest, until there was no one left except her, the scepter, and the legion of guards flanking Queen Karen.

Queen Karen snatched the scepter out of Queen Ebon's hands. And with that, the water ceased. There wasn't a single shelter left standing. Queen Ebon crumpled inside, for her people, every last one, were gone. She tried to explain what happened to Queen Karen, to Enilder, but it was too late. The land was destroyed.

I asked, "Which queen do you think was the worst ruler?" but my daughter's eyes were closed by then. She was fast asleep before I could finish, but she will get it soon.

Maybe you will too.

Be a wall
A barbed-wire fortress
Someone will still try to climb.

Catching Flies

Maybe you have ascribed these stories to delusion? I would argue that there is a fine line between one god's delusion and another one's wisdom. Still, I have not always been this wise. I was once green and gullible too. Believed love to be the magic of closed-mouth kisses and unpressed bodies. Then, somewhere, like a sleight of the hand, that knowing became another.

I don't even remember my mother giving me "the talk." I just figured lovemaking was done upside down. Like it was back when the world was flat and lush. Sixty million years ago. Our prehensile toes curled around the branches. Our open mouths. A forceful ejection of tongues. The sticky roar of ground lions drunk off the absinthe of each other. Us, hallucinating until our skin was colorless. Become one thing. Gold leaf. Abalone. Violent kaleidoscope. Hypoglossal rhythm of thunderstone. Bodies in black light. Where we see each other and do not flinch. How we tear our skin on each other's bones. And die while we are too young to regret it.

I guess even then I reckoned Love and Death to be tightly wound. And maybe nothing is closer to the truth. That naivety offers us a murderous hand. Maybe that was what our mothers were warning us of all those years. That the thirst of Love can lead us into desperate places.

My grandmother used to take me out to the garden in the corner of the yard and teach me how to sow. How to wait for something to surprise the earth. Decades ago, every family had a garden. Every garden had a story. Some planted by great-greats whose only pride was found in the autograph of grape vines on lattices in a ground that they owned. Others, the art of nature taking back abandoned plots after folks had died and the heirs had left them to ruin. But this world used to be an urban paradise. Handlaid brick that met fresh-tilled soil. Tomatoes haloed in chicken wire. Ida Mae's utopia.

Better Than Nothing

My great-great-grandma Ida Mae would pull her oxygen tank, with the eighty-foot cord, out to where the melons swelled and the lizards stayed full, singing the new buds into full blossom. Her apron shielding her bare legs from the thorns. There, the sun would kiss her skin and life would grow from the ground. Sometimes in unexpected places.

One day, amid the wild grass and turnip greens, Ida Mae noticed a new luminescent saffron tucked warm against the earth. She pulled back the frantic leaves only to find a seed had taken root. A gourd, unlike the warted orbs that tangled around the chain-link divider. This one, slender round the breasts and curvaceously hipped, sat like a goddess shimmering in the afternoon gleam. The tendrils fading into a shadow of ripe. Ida Mae pulled her shears from her apron and clipped the new harvest. She smiled. The sun now readying to set, she returned to the house with thoughts of summer soups and compotes for the local farmer's market.

Sitting the pear-obelisk on the counter, she went to retrieve a knife to gut out all the flavor for her pan. Before she could slice, a low thud startled her. Across the kitchen, she saw the gourd begin to shake, the dull of a knock accompanying each rock. She clutched the knife and inched closer. The gourd shed its husk, and in the seedy middle sat a fully developed baby. Ida Mae, well into her years, had no desire for a child. Her children had children who had grown and been long gone into their own endeavors. The baby saw the confusion in her face and became a fountain of tears. Ida Mae, the way mothers do, put her feelings away and brought the baby to her chest. She kissed her on her forehead and hushed her sweet Dolores to peace. From that day, they were inseparable.

Ida Mae would take her out to the garden and teach her how to tell when the greens were ready to pull or how peppermint oil would push away the fire ants in the spring. She ate every word and, just like a gourd, grew bigger and bigger until she stood thigh high to Ida Mae. Her wild hair danced with southern sweat, and her skin toasted to a berry-black tint. Dolores, belly round like a child before a growth spurt, now old enough to sing her own song, began trying to test Ida Mae's limits. Dolores would sneak into the garden and eat handfuls of blackberries off the bush before dinner; the worst way to ruin your appetite, Ida Mae would say. Then, when asked if she did it, Dolores would look her straight in the eye, blue-black-seed-dotted smile, and profess *No* as boldly as she had eaten. But there is one thing you should know about gourd babies: when they lie, they shrink a little, not just on the outside. So at the end of every day Ida Mae would bring Dolores and stand her up against the doorframe and mark her height in pencil on the woodgrain to see how truthful she had been. Every inch she was smaller at the end of the day warranted another swift swat with the switch.

Dolores learned quickly the dangers of weaving webs of lies. So by the time she was a young woman, she stood a head above Ida Mae's curling body in the garden. They discussed pruning back the peach trees and the importance of encroaching. Dolores knew too well the idea of being pushed back. She tired of living under the rule of her mother's outdated curfews. Though she loved her, she wanted to see the world for herself. Ida Mae had no desire to hold on to things that she couldn't help. Though she would miss the companionship, she wanted so much for Dolores. And if she felt it was time to go, Ida Mae wasn't going to stand in her way. But Ida Mae warned Dolores to always be honest with herself. And if she ever needed to return home, Ida Mae would be there with open arms. Dolores promised, both knowing the cruelty of the world and the risks of one too many fibs.

Determined to prove her own independence, Dolores got a job working at a diner in town. She rented herself a fancy apartment with her first check. Before long, she was helping in the kitchen, offering new twists on old dishes with her knowledge from the garden. Then, one day, a suave-skinned man in a tailored pin-striped suit sat at the end of the counter, waving his long pretty fingers at Dolores. Robert. She was smitten. He ordered every drink they had on the menu one by one so Dolores would have to keep coming back to serve him. He made her laugh in ways her belly didn't know it could. When he was done, he asked for the bill, and she wrote down her number. They spent the next three months fastened to the phone. They would talk from when the owl hooed to when the rooster cocked, only taking breaks to go to their respective jobs. She knew it was meant to be, so when Robert got down on one knee in the middle of the church bazaar, she couldn't say yes fast enough. But Ida Mae had reservations.

Nearing her final matchup with Death, Ida Mae saw more clearly. She saw Dolores slipping from her own independence.

And something down in Robert's heart unsettled her. She warned Dolores to be careful, but Dolores was so taken with Robert that she brushed it off as Ida Mae's old age. The night before they jumped the broom, Dolores started to have cold feet. What if Ida Mae was right? What if Robert wasn't the kind of man she could build her own garden with? She paced back and forth until the weariness of it all knocked her clean off her feet. She reconciled her anxiety, that it was all for nothing. She knew who he was. And she loved him. Everything would be fine.

The next day, she woke with the joy of matrimony filling her heart. Her bridesmaids helped wrap her in the white taffeta dress and adorn her hair with lilies from Ida Mae's garden. But when Dolores began to walk down the aisle, she stumbled over her dress, like there was more of it than before. The tailor must have mismeasured. Her bridesmaids quickly pinned the underskirt, and Dolores made it down the aisle. After the kiss, the cake, and the dance, Robert and Dolores began to build their home together.

At first, Robert would come home every night before the sun danced its way across the horizon. But after the first month, he would go missing for days. Each time blaming work or a miscalculation of time. Then, he would bring her flowers and apologize, only to go missing again the very next day. She knew home was only a short ride away, but what would Ida Mae say? How could she face her now? Who would she be without him? She would quickly tell herself that everyone compromises in marriage, and wash any thoughts of being homebound out. A foot lost in the first year.

To busy her mind from the hollow halls of her heart, she picked up extra shifts at the diner. She found the busy clank of dishes and the smiles of regulars a comforting break from the loneliness. Unfortunately, the ever-demanding needs of a short-staffed eatery constantly put her in need. Her dependability only served as a further burden. Before long, the manager was scheduling her for longer and longer shifts, specifically those that stretched into the wee hours of the morning. The restaurant would empty, outside of beggars and truckers making their way through town. Dolores didn't want to clock out in the darkest hours, but if she didn't, who would? Besides, her paycheck would be big enough to afford something nice, right? Maybe nice enough to bring Robert back home. Shrink. I mean, her boss didn't intend to take advantage of her; she just saw that Dolores was a hard worker. Shrink.

Before long Dolores needed a step stool just to reach the cash register. Between the baggy clothes and rude remarks of late-night transients, she thought of herself every so often. She would catch a glimpse in the window chalk, a figurine in frame. She would try not to look too closely for fear that Ida Mae would sense the shame and think to call. Dolores figured she was far too busy in her garden to care anyhow. No point in visiting just to become a failure in graphite against the wooden frame. But by the time the leaves began to find their sorcery, shape-shifting into muted pigments of burgundy and orange, the need to see Ida Mae again was gnawing at her heart. Maybe it was just a longing for home. Maybe it was the day that Robert returned to find her now knee-high body desperately waiting by the window for him. The day he left with more bags than excuses. Some things are just too small to love.

Her body now the master of its own fate, she didn't even remember calling a ride. Her doll arms attempted to pull herself up to look out the window as they turned onto the dusty road that led to Ida Mae's house.

She hopped down from the car, racing to her mother's door. She banged her small knuckles against the wood as hard as she could, but no one answered. She tried the door, but it was locked. She found a way to shimmy up into the window, only to see a house frozen. All of Ida Mae's things intact, but no sign of her. She must've been in the garden. Dolores ran as fast as her stumpy legs could take her. Past the side porch where she and Ida Mae used to snap beans for Sunday dinner, around the old shed where all her Christmas gifts tried to hide, through the iron gate that led to the wild tendrils and the unruly vines.

There, right where Ida Mae would stand with one hand on her hip surveying the lot of bell peppers and turnip greens, it stood. Round around the top, the stone was almost as tall as Dolores. The earth had known it for a while. You could tell by the way the green tangled its arms around the smooth sides like a daughter. Ida Mae's name in script, dates only a few months in the making. Dolores pressed her hand to the granite angel guarding the plot and began to shudder. She was not herself, she had not been for longer than she would've liked to admit. An apology. She pressed her back into the stone and filled her lap with the dry petals of forgotten roses. Then she told Ida Mae how she didn't spend one minute missing her, over and over, until she was the size of a seed. One finally home in the dark soil and the green swath. Hoping to grow. Grow into something big. Big enough to love.

And this is the beginning of the first path to Death, for there are many. This is the kind of longing that lingers around us. The kind that boasts of its ability to out-suffer. Makes us give our hearts away too easily. The kind that sees it all but drives past every red flag. The first kind we are taught to chase. We both know that Love seeks those with accommodating hearts. And to show that you can ride, even into Death's arms, that you can keep secrets, that if you don't ask questions, you can't be responsible for the guilty answer. Call it ride or die. This version of mercy I'm sure the gods approve.

Since my parents spent so much time at the church, my friend group consisted of other pastors' children, deacons' children, grandchildren of sanctified grandmothers, or children I met at pastoral anniversaries and celebrations around the desert. Often, we would meet up while all our parents shared counseling sessions or were deep in their own worship. For every god has a god. We would try to keep our patchwork relationships going from chance meeting to chance meeting, but most times fell short, since we weren't old enough to drive. On one or two occasions, our parents would schedule us preteen playdates, where they would trade off the responsibility of offering us snacks while we played outside or watched a movie on someone's couch. That is how I met Ashley.

One day, in Bible study, we hit it off. We spent the time during the potluck after church laughing it up and talking about how things worked at our respective schools. She said she had already started dating, but the pool at her school was so shallow she began fishing at neighboring high schools. She was pretty, brown-skinned and slim but with curves everyone noticed. But more than that, there was an air of confidence about her, one only gained through experiences my parents warned me not to seek out. Ones T and Monique had mastered, maybe too well. Maybe this was the reason we never had a real relationship outside of T pretending I was the daughter she already had. She spent more time trying to spank me than she ever spent teaching me all the lessons that she learned the hard way. Maybe that is what intrigued me most about the magic of boys. They had a mysterious danger that called to me, even though I knew all that it could change.

Ashley scrolled through her phone, showing me all the names of boys she knew and offering to hook me up with one if I was interested. I was interested. Ever since we all watched both of my sisters bring home babies before diplomas, my parents kept me as far away from magic as possible. My twelve-year-old sensibilities were shifting from Foursquare to investigating how to make that smacking noise couples in the movies make when they kiss. Lately, the crudeness of the familiar boys had started to wane. Like a film falling from my eyes, something beckoning me to straighten my locs and drape a dress around my nonexistent curves, but I had no idea how to start. Ashley's invitation seemed like a great first step. She pulled out her purse and started to show me pictures that boys had given her to remember them. This was back when Glamour Shots in every mall welcomed the picking of sunburst backgrounds with your friends. Small mementos bulging from pockets as each Monday welcomed a ritual of photo drops to those who your heart thought of all weekend. It was somewhat of a status symbol to see how many pictures you were given, and Ashley had a purse full. Some tall. Some short. Then she landed on this one image: milk-chocolate boy with pretty gray eyes. He wore a white shirt that smelled fresh against his dark skin even through the picture. Atop his head sat a wide-brimmed conical hat made for shade in the rice fields—a "Chinaman hat," or at least that's what she called it. I remember my heart in full flutter as I asked his name.

"Michael," she said.

Michael with the Chinese hat. I remember how good his name felt on my lips, like an angel from Heaven in full descent. And God looked at him and knew it was good.

"Can you introduce us?" I shyly asked.

"Of course! Why don't you ask your mom if you can come by my house on Saturday? My mom will make us some food and we can watch movies."

I tried to control my smile as it spread wide across my face. I didn't want to seem too eager. And I needed a way to undo my sisters' tainting in my parents' minds of anyone dating before age thirty. I tried to play it cool. Waited until my mother was full of praise before asking if I could go hang out at Ashley's. In a strange twist of Mercury's rotation, she agreed without further prodding. No typical fourth degree, or surrendering my companion's parents' social security numbers, full names, addresses, and birthdates. I took it as a sign that me and Michael with the Chinese hat must be meant to meet. Maybe I should've known then that it was nothing but the dragon's orchestration.

I held my breath all week for Saturday to come. I lined the foot of my bed with outfit choices, examining each one in the light. Convinced my baby hair to give itself over to the authority of Pro Styl. Then lost myself to a daydream. One where I walked into the room and Michael with the Chinese hat's eyes were bound to my body. Us, sitting too close for adult comfort, leaning in. And if I dared, even . . . kissing!

But this thought must stay secret. If my parents caught any wind of my plans, they would be over before they started.

When the day came, my mother drove me to Ashley's, making small talk as we turned down the dusty boulevard.

"So what are you girls gonna get into today?"

"Just watching some movies. Maybe playing in her backyard." I tried to stay cool. Hoped that she had not sensed something by the way my body was slathered in Love Spell.

She had plenty of time to ask questions as we coasted deeper into the Empire's cul-de-sac valley. The houses becoming more uniform. The rooftops inching so close you could jump from one to another. Each window close enough to run a string and cup to the next and telephone a friend the childish way. My mother always hated those neighborhoods. Said the houses were so close that if you sneezed in your bathroom you could hear the neighbor say "bless you" in their kitchen. But I saw each cookie-cutter home as a step closer and closer to the boy I may one day love. And farther and farther from my mother's interrogation. By the time we arrived, I had assured her that girl time was going to be in full effect. Not a hint of boy charm in sight.

I hopped out while the motor was still running. My prepaid cell tucked in my pocket. She told me to call her whenever I was done. She also told me to tell Ashley's mom thank you, and I promised I would. I trembled up to the door and knocked until I heard footsteps approaching. Ashley creaked the door open.

"Hey! Come on in." She closed the door behind her. "The boys will be here soon."

I took a deep breath and attempted to find the perfect way to perch myself in the room for my first impression. I asked Ashley where her mom was so I could thank her.

"Oh, my mom isn't here," she replied.

"What do you mean?" I asked. "I thought the plan was food and movies."

"She had to work, but don't worry, she left money for pizza."

She spoke like being home alone didn't warrant another level of caution. A calm I didn't know how to navigate. This you must know was the dragon's claw. I see it clearly in hindsight. Maybe then my gut knew too.

My mother's mantra began ringing in my head— "Nobody in and nobody out"—but what was I going to do, call her and ask her to come back? Ruin what image I had left? What story could I weave out of an empty driveway and a couch full of boys? Maybe this was not my doing. Maybe I was a victim of Ashley's trick. Maybe the facts would be enough. I looked out the window to see if my mother had cleared the block, but she was nowhere in sight.

Another breath. This one more intoxicating than the last. I drank my own pride and reckoned, who was I to fear Love? A young woman with all her fortifications intact. A blossoming vine taking over an entire rampart. I knew I was ready to lock him in my arms, and how dare he want to get out. Then I noticed Ashley's skirt was much shorter than I had seen her wear before. On closer examination, it looked like she swept her mother's makeup drawer clean with her face. She was all grown, with nowhere to go. Doubt began to spread out in my chest. I shifted on the barstool, readjusting the flower barrette pinning back my afro puff. Ashley danced in and out of the room with a new accessory every trip—until the doorbell finally rang.

My heart leapt up. I adjusted my training bra and fixed my clothes. The first boy to enter was on Ashley like cold ketchup on a warm fry. He draped his arms around her as she lifted her legs to crisscross around his midsection. He lifted her with ease and slid his tongue to lick the salt in the back of her throat. Behind him, all evenly melted and brown, poured in a beam of toasted light. I hardly recognized him without the straw pagoda on top of his head, but it was him. I knew by the piercing gray eyes. That was Michael.

I readjusted my clothes again, hoping he couldn't see that I was young and new to all of this. Ashley introduced us, and he shook my soft and limp hand in his, the way my daddy always said not to. My grandfather had drilled in him, and he had drilled in me, that a firm handshake lets people know you mean business. But I was instantly Play-Doh in Michael's hands. Ashley showed us to the converted garage.

In it there was a medium-size box of a TV set up in front of a futon and a small love seat. She told us to settle in, and she and her friend would get us some snacks and drinks. Then she left me and Michael alone to get more acquainted.

I wanted to know everything about him: what school he went to, his favorite TV shows. What were his hobbies? Did he have siblings? After all, if we were going to be together forever, like I knew we were meant to be, we would have to move fast. So I kicked us off:

"So, Michael, what school do you go to?" I stammered out.

Then his lips slowed. All the sound dropped out. The saliva danced across his full lips as they pulled apart like two full wings ready to take flight and then descended back into themselves with the same bated breath. The bass of his voice caressed my ear. He sat closer and closer, until his arm was around me the way I'd seen boys do in the movies. His chest was pressed against my side, and he was leaning in. I closed my eyes for my first kiss and then suddenly felt his split tongue slithering all over my neck. I opened my eyes and jumped back, startled. His eyes widened, and his smile started to spread like a plague.

"Come here, girl." He whispered like he was trying to sell me something no one else wanted to buy.

Then the uneasy rose. I urged him to slow down, but he just kept advancing. I leaned back. His claws gripped the knobs of my chest, turning them like he intended to open me up. We fell to the floor. He was on top of me with my hands pinned between his body and mine. I called for Ashley, but she didn't come. I called louder—still no answer. I felt the earth beneath me quake as he slid his claws underneath my thighs and tried to come for the salt in the back of my throat. I threw him off me. He pinned my wrists with his talons. We tousled around the garage like two birds caught in a rafter until I finally landed a clean hit to the side of his head. He called me a bitch, but I had escaped out the door. I heard him thrashing about the garage as I ran to the back of the house.

Ashley's door was locked. A repeating thud played amid the broken record of her giggle. I knocked harder, tried to tell her through the door what happened. The thudding paused just long enough for me to feel heat from the other side of the door. She said I should "stop being scared" and "give him what he wants." It was clear she harbored her own talons. I backed away from her room and headed for the front door. I stood in the yard with tears streaming down my face, trying to get it all out before I called my mother. But I wasn't going to stay there and wait for either of them to come get me, so I started walking. A few houses down, I finally got up the nerve to call. I bumbled out something about a disagreement and then asked to be saved.

I stumbled down the street, the houses spreading farther apart than before. I ducked and dodged between the trees of the undeveloped lots until I was sure they weren't following me. I waved my mom's van down a few blocks up. She greeted me and could immediately see I was shaken.

"I just don't want to talk about it."

My mother tightened her knuckles around the steering wheel, as if it was my childlike hand that she knew she had to eventually let go. Every daughter has their fall to bear. She wasn't going to chase me. All she could hope is that I would eventually run back to her and let the tears stain her chest while she wrapped me in a song. Instead, I stared out the window, counting the trees like witnesses who could be called on later to testify. Though I knew I could never tell anyone how I had run. I would have to swallow this whole thing with Michael like wet concrete, or I would never get to see another boy again. For the dragon is more than an urban legend. Swallow its name too many times and it will make a mockery of you. Make you its midnight itch that it is sure to scratch. I wish that was the only time the dragon tried hoarding a part of me. But when seeking the smell of fire, there are far too many other things that sell you on their burn.

College was a blur, but not for the reasons you may think. I enrolled at seventeen. I was awkward, young, and intent on removing myself from much of the tomfoolery that comes with being out on your own for the first time. I settled in with my core group of guy friends. I have always found that hanging with guys has less pressure than their female counterparts. They can be in an all-out brawl and, in the next breath, reconcile over a drink. It is amazing to me the amount of humanness that can be forgiven in a matter of moments. Unfortunately, I was always in the friend zone. No matter how many meals I cooked, homework help I offered, love advice I gave, I was always "Momma." I resolved that the right man would one day interpret my nurturing and caring nature as a sexy attribute. Until then, I decided to focus on my studies. And somehow those studies landed me on a campus forty-five minutes outside the City of Motors, but still close enough to sneak down to the auto show on the weekends. The small college town only existed because of the university that sat at its center. The streets bled an oil-slick maize and blue that greased the weather with more defined seasons than I ever knew in the Empire. The City of Motors knew how to callous a hand, how to frostbite an exposed lip, knew spit, grind, grit, and rev, but I loved the challenge of even being a stone's throw away. And in some ways, maybe that pushed me even harder to manufacture a win on campus. I found myself taking classes that were way outside any classification I ever thought would interest me. I guess that's how I stumbled into a course offered in the Linguistics Department my sophomore year: African American English.

The professor was a Bubba Sparxxx doppelganger dressed in a tailored suit, with the accent to match. He wore thick Coke-bottle glasses. He was the ultimate paradox. His doctorate may have been in linguistics, but his love for Black culture permeated every analogy. He stood at the front of the class, watching as the room lost negative space. The white students filing in one by one, settling into their desks. I sat near the back, center of the room, the ink blot in the sea of cream. I kept myself to silence, having learned it is not always best to show your wisdom at the first hand.

Finally, another drop of ink is stirred into the room. And Black he was. The kind of Black my mother refers to as Blue-Black. A midnight-chocolate shorty with a fitted cap cocked to the side and a swagger that definitely didn't come from the Region of Great Lakes that spread between here and the nearby City of Motors. Ironically, his name was Alabaster, but everyone called him Bas. He smelled of a cherry Black and Mild and purple Kool-Aid familiarity that made me miss visiting my friends in the projects near the heart of the Empire. A few more students made their way in to fill the classroom. Lastly walked in Brandon, star football player with a girl on his arm. She looked so proud to have stuck his forecasted Heisman nomination so far up her skirt that she couldn't see straight. Everyone moved for him. He sat near us, made eye contact, and gave a nod. She sat near him and didn't speak. She was model pretty, the kind of Black girl who carries a designer backpack and wears heels in the snow. I could imagine her in a catfight in a club on Bell Isle because someone "looked at her man wrong." When they called roll, she was never mentioned, but she turned her nose up whenever we caught eyes.

The professor began introducing the course. He explained that linguistically African American Vernacular English, also known as Ebonics, has its own rules and laws. This semester we would unpack how they are used and attempt to master their contextual implications.

Bas leaned over to me with a huge, gapped-tooth smile and said, "I have been doing this my whole life! This is going to be cake!"

We instantly realized that every white person around us seemed baffled. Like the thought that all our back-of-hand slapping and slang could actually be a dialect of the Queen's English was astonishing.

Over the next few months, Bas and I begin to meld into something like a finished sentence. The only two students in the class taking out emergency loans to make our tuition payments, spending two days a week as the star student examples of how to balance poverty and the use of the "habitual been." I mean we *been* struggling for years, so it came to us like a native tongue. Brandon was barely there. His girl came in with her nose held high and took notes for him. There was a rumor that the entire football team had an automatic A in every subject because they made the school so much money. To dispel that, every once in a while, Brandon showed up and took a quiz or a test. The girl with the high nose always by his side, running to get a drink at a hint of a tickle in his throat. I have always despised women like her. She was the kind that abandoned her own success for him. I bet she betted on being his trophy wife. A bent moral. A hidden face in a sea of his wrongdoing. I bet she blew her future on a roulette bet that he would enter the draft. I bet he had a million of her hidden all over campus just waiting to be seen. I tried to contain my disgust.

On another note, Bas and I had started spending time outside of class "studying." He was weekend easy all the time. My cheeks hurt from laughter every day that I was with him, but we weren't "together." No matter how much I wanted to be. He was there trying to get back on football scholarship after an injury, but I knew he had plans to leave. I wanted him to stay. I never saw him outside of class during the day, but we texted all day long. It was a big campus, I reasoned. He arrived when the sky matched his skin, spent late nights with me at the university radio station shit-talking, rhyming, and laughing with the night-show host. I was another version of myself with him. It was like he saw through all my layers, knew me at my core, called me by my name. And I let my guard down.

One day, he asked to take me to lunch at his favorite sandwich shop in the suburb over. I gushed at the idea of being with him. He picked me up in his old sedan, a Monte Carlo or maybe an Oldsmobile. He finished a cherry Black as I crawled into the passenger side, and he let a ring of smoke billow from his mouth. Then he leaned over and kissed me on the cheek. He said he needed to make a stop before we left. I stared out the window watching the white students head for the student union to congregate as usual.

As we pulled up on the side street, his voice changed to urgency. He tossed me his hoodie and commanded me to put it on. Before I could adjust it, he yanked the hood over my head and barked for me not to look in the back seat. I sunk down into a ball as we slowed to a stop. I didn't know what was going on, but something told me to be small and forgettable. He cut his eyes at me. This was not the man that I had known for weeks, or maybe it was. Either way, he wanted me invisible, so I was. The back door opened and a body jumped in. My heart wanted to be quiet and to be his. I didn't know how to be both. I tried not to question, but my responsibility wouldn't let me stay blind. I tried to see out of the side mirror, but whatever was happening wasn't directly behind me. I glanced up slightly at the bottom of the rearview mirror and saw Bas extend his hand with his thumb tucked against his palm. A green and cellophane secret slipped between them. There was an exchange and then the door opened and closed and we were alone again. He pulled the hood from my head and brushed my hair back with his hand. Then whispered, "I am sorry I had to put you in all of that. Are you ready to eat?"

I thought about condemnation. To tell him how much danger he was putting himself in. To tell him how uncomfortable I was. Then I thought of Brandon's girl. I wonder how many of his secrets she held. How he rode back to her again and again like a dedicated wave. Tuition was due, I justified. This was probably a one-time thing. He threw his arm around me like a brazen idol. I couldn't remember my name, but I was his. Was this enough to quantify as Love? I dare believe everyone whose heart is big enough to hide something has convinced ourselves of that. Submission can be its own death of self.

Maybe I speak of this path to Death too soon. For I have yet to tell you of her inner workings. History has been shown to have a tendency to take things out of context. And I fear you have met Acirema's hand too often to take me at my word. Still, maybe I am too subscribed to Hope to hold back. I have shown you that I have known some version of Love, if that's what you were to call it. But in order to truly understand my ways, you must first abandon what you know of Death. She is not what you have learned.

Daughter of Paradise's Fall. Mother of Permanent Peace. Home Caller. Memory Thief. Sallie Mae of Souls. The Forgetless Rememberer. Heaven's Final Concierge aka Light at Tunnel's End aka Reincarnation's Right Hand aka Eternal Midwife aka Anesthesiologist to the Afterlife. The Ghost Surrenderer. The Church Mother in Demise's Sanctuary. The Dragon's Aftermath. Collector of Last Breaths and First Revelations. The Great Transcender. The Lord of Beckoning. Amen. Death Herself was born in Fear.

Her first cry, the kind of paralysis that comes only at the

boundary of blood and soul. Her father, Azrael, her mother, Eden. What harsh things we spark behind the back of God. Their bodies rough, moss and stripped flint, fucked a wildfire. Found among the ashes. Round and Black. Rose like an ember and just as radiant. Her mother draped her in a cloak of midnight blue to hide her from Envy. But the cloak gained its own power. Finding all the lost faces, the ones too scared of the life that left them. They say it held a million souls the first day. Two million by the second. Hungry. Heavily fusing to her skin, refusing to forget a name. The grief sat in her dimples like open graves. Built her a mausoleum smile. So heavy, she craved neither breast nor bottle, but sucked her mother's spirit dry. Knew life so close she could take it. Brimstone touch, even when she didn't mean to burn. She was grown strong and alone enough to know Fear like it was home.

On her ninth birthday, her father gave her a gentle elephant and an onyx scythe. Both too heavy for mortal hands. Told her it was time to work. The way all our bodies cannot avoid. To guard the in-between with no way to move back in time. To make sure none linger here. Where her cloak soaks in the moments that our minds work to forget. What a burden to remember everything and have no way to fix it. She looks for someone to hold her hand. Dare to look deep. The way the ageless invite the tomb. To say there is a peace in her eyes. Not just a flash of life. Somewhere they want to stay. Forever.

Maybe this is the knowledge I should have been bequeathing you all along. Maybe what you needed was not a march but a martyr. A cross to co-bear. For me to tell you all the ways I have died. And all the ways I have been reborn. Maybe it is time I tell you more about the dragon.

This time when we met, Bas and I had been entwined for almost a month. I hadn't been keeping track of time. But that's how winters in the Region of Great Lakes work. The long days stretch into dark icy nights. People stay to themselves, inside as much as possible. They hunker down when the snow piles high and resort to Pizza House for daily sustenance. I live too far across campus to seek out any council of friends. But Bas draws me to his warmth every chance I get.

I did have one close connection. A girl named Kathia I met at ladies' night at the union pool hall and quickly befriended. She lived across campus, which was not a big surprise. I was one of maybe five women with skin dark enough to live centrally. It seemed as though they picked one ethnic name per floor for diversity. Every other -isha or -ia was on North Campus, a bus ride away. Kathia wasn't as fortunate.

Her dad was rich. A Middle Eastern businessman who kept her well outfitted with the nicest UGGs and the best perks. After dinner one evening, she told me that she had four tickets to see the Pistons play the Lakers at the Auburn Palace. I hated the Pistons but have been a woman of purple and gold royalty for longer than I could breathe. Plus, I wanted to see the inside of the Palace. Analyze its wealth and worthiness. Compare it to my own queendom. I decided it was time to dust off my Derek Fisher jersey from the last three-peat buzzer win, even if I was the only fan in the audience. She asked if I knew anyone who had a car who might want to go. I knew exactly who to ask.

Bas was ecstatic. He even invited his friend Rashad to join us. I'd met Rashad once before as part of one of Bas's romantic late-night gestures. He didn't speak much, hung in the shadow like an icicle in the window that slowly melted onto everything. We figured we could hook him up with Kathia, call it a double date. Decided we were all going to meet up before the game to grab a bite and then head out. The Palace was over an hour's drive, but to get away from campus before midterms was a beautiful treat we welcomed.

We all met at the student union. The boys were late, so Kathia and I grabbed a quick bite before they got there. Bas called me from the car to say he was outside. We trudged through the snow and black ice to warm our bodies against the cloth seats as fast as possible. When we got in, I hugged Bas, absorbing all the heat from his skin. He introduced Kathia to Rashad, whose legs took up most of the back seat. From his seated position, we couldn't tell if he was a terrible spreader or taller than life. He wasn't old, but older than us. His furrowed brow told of hard winters and past-due bills. His large lips sat wide over his gap-tooth smile that was almost endearing. Kathia tried to navigate space around his body but ended up with her small frame crammed to one side. They all stopped and stared at me. I then realized that everyone else had on Pistons gear. Bas laughed and said the fans were going to "murder" me, but then he promised to protect me.

We spent the next over-an-hour cracking jokes, singing songs loudly, and talking shit about the game. When we arrived, the sun was setting and the only parking space we could find put us in peril of black ice, snow mounds, and frostbite. We tried to bundle up. Bas tucked his hands in my side pockets and waddled behind me, trusting me to lead the way, since I was built for harsh weather. Kathia and Rashad tried to make it visually known that they were *not* together. Our hope for a faithful foursome went out the window as they drifted farther into the flurries. Once we entered in from the cold, the other Piston fans passed us, casting harsh stares like we were covered in filth. Well, stared at me like I was. Bas thought it was hilarious and constantly made jokes about how he "shoulda left me at home with all that."

We started the ascent to our seats. We figured, with Kathia's dad's status, we shouldn't have had to climb for long. We were wrong. Before we knew it, we had scaled an entire mountain, landing in the nosebleeds at the top of the Palace. Every player looked like a toy figurine. We saw there were some additional seats in a closer section, so we decided we would take the risk of sitting there. If the attendees showed up, we vowed we would move without provocation. We got comfortable in the tiny folding seats. Rashad sat on the end to stretch his mile-long legs out into the aisle. Kathia refused to sit next to him, so Bas took his cue. Then Kathia sat down beside me. Every time the Lakers scored, I stood and clapped, garnering all the dirty looks I could hold. Unfortunately, around the fourth quarter, I found myself standing less, and before I knew it, the game was over and every fan around me was smiling and shooting their condescending looks in my direction.

We headed out. People giggled and pointed to my jersey as I sulked in defeat. We walked out through the frigid, dark chill and headed toward the car. When we climbed in, Kathia made sure to get in first, staking her claim along the back seat, forcing Rashad to sit on his hip just to fit. She seemed happier the entire ride back. When we got to campus, Bas offered to take Kathia back up north if she wanted to hang out a little longer. After a certain hour, the buses only ran every hour and they were rarely on time. Waiting out in the cold only made room for sickness. She said she couldn't stay long but lingered, talking and playing spades deep into the dark hours. Eventually, she announced that she was ready to turn in so she could make it to class on time. Bas convinced me to stick around until he got back. Said Rashad would be leaving soon and promised me warmth that only two bodies can make. I couldn't resist his heat. I settled in on his bed to watch TV as he headed out to brave the cold. Rashad and I awkwardly tried to strike up a conversation. It ended with him sitting at the foot of the bed texting somebody and laughing to himself. I lay horizontally across the bed and ended up drifting off to sleep. I guess I underestimated how long the trip across campus would take. Before I knew it, I was in a dream.

There was a large, lush field rolled out in front of me. A yield of yellow lady's slippers. A sea of Dutchman's-breeches. I tiptoed through them, trying not to crush a single bud. I was struck by the sight of a large Dragon tree at the horizon line. It seemed to reach Heaven and know its wonders. I began to run to it, when I saw its arms begin to bend. They extended toward me. I was initially in awe of how it wanted me closer, but its arms increased in number. The sky darkened; then the temperature dropped. I was full of dread. My chest tightened. No longer in tropical spring, the tundra and its crystallized arms doubled faster and faster. I ran for the well at the opposite horizon. My feet lost traction as I slipped across the icy terrain looking for some shelter from the blizzard or the hunt. I reached the lip of the well, where a rope sat. I tied it to my waist. The encroaching branches gained speed. I straddled the brick, my feet slipping on the inside of the well as I rappelled down. The sky creaked to utter disquietude. My feet splashed into the water, and I could go no farther. I was in an abyss, dangling from a rope, and it was the kind of quiet that mothers fear. Then there was a pull, and another. By the third pull, I came to, and it was back-alley dark.

I was uncharacteristically sleeping on my back when a shadow, broad and intentional, lingered over me. Then another tug. The rope had now turned into my belt. It was stuck, and the shadow yanked like it was taking back something it was owed. I reached to grab for it only to feel a soft, unfamiliar lump dangling on the back of my hand. The belt pulled, and my vision cleared to see it was Rashad. He was stark naked and on top of me. His breath billowing frost into the air. The moonlight caught his bark-brown skin as he tried to pull my pants free, but the belt was caught. He yanked. He didn't realize I was awake. I was alone, feigning sleep, the way a possum lies under the drooling mouth of its predator.

I felt the window to escape closing. I put my hands to his chest and pushed like I was trying to move a frozen stump by myself. Caught off guard by my consciousness, he fell off the bed and onto the floor. I had just enough time to grab my keys and phone from the bed and feel my way to the door. I felt his hand vine around my ankle, but I was too fast. And before he could stand, I was free. I broke for outside, down the long winding corridor.

I stood in the thick of winter. The campus was asleep. I pulled my hoodie up over my ears, tucked my hands under my armpits, and made my way toward home. I could not control my heartbeat in this village of dragons. My breath was a constant blast of white as I kept checking behind me to see if he was following. I ducked down a side street that cut the chill that was slicing through my chest. Then there was a vibration that resonated from my back pocket, up my spine, and I felt him crawling on me all over again. My phone rang. It was Bas.

The words and tears swirled together to make an undiscovered sound from my mouth.

"He tried . . . He tried . . ."

"What did he try?!" he replied sharply.

I wanted to tell him. But the words were an ice cube going down the wrong way.

The next semester Bas transferred. I never saw Rashad again. But every time I passed the dorm, I could feel the chill, the gripping sensation that someone was following me, asking me to prove it ever happened.

We all have evidence in our minds. One no court would admit. The dragons bet on this loophole. For they cannot be charged with murder if they do not kill. They are not as kind as Death. They do far worse. They shame. I do not think you yet understand how shame blisters. How being burned by it leaves you forever, in part, disabled. For ice can burn as badly as fire. And dragons have a way of freezing everything. Hypothermia of the heart.

Still, better one dragon than the one with three heads. The one who knows what it is to have your skin scale over but still chooses to desolate her own den. By force or by omission. The Hydra has her own bloodline, though I hesitate to call her a mother. One of the women who traded sight for denial—call it their own heirloom. They stayed after the Great Flight too. Teach us all that it is only reasonable to run to Death when you have been tangled in three tongues, all promising to be writhing out of Love. This one, the Hydra, may be the worst dragon yet.

I was supposed to stay at Nee Nee's house once I landed in the Mile High City. We met competing at one of the largest poetry slams. She seemed down to earth and was an accomplished performer whose name evoked an audible reaction from the audience. I was young and still making my name familiar. She and a group of powerhouse female poets welcomed me in. I don't know if she saw something in me or just liked the way I performed, but we ended up sharing meals and then late-night cyphers in our hotel rooms. At every turn, she found a way to offer an encouraging word or a critique that made the work better. After placing in a few competitions and several nights spent dancing the moon down to Black Eyed Peas, she reached out to me and offered to take me around. Show me all that the Mile High City had to offer a writer like me. I was so excited just to be going somewhere. I jumped at the chance to see a new skyline, especially one that boasted of boulder cities, whitewater summers, and sat at the top of the world like it floated on a bed of clouds. It was hard to breath in the Mile High City, but most people confused that with euphoria. And there was a certain kind of mysticism about it. Somewhere lodged in the weed-smoking culture or the quaint coffee shops that served hookah. Things this far up seemed more relaxed. Easy.

Nee Nee embraced me in a hug at the security gate like we were long-lost family. She asked me about my flight in, wanted to see if I was hungry before we hit the road. There was little time to grab anything before my first scheduled gig at a local coffee shop. With no time to drop my luggage off, we just took everything with us and headed out. Nee Nee got me to my first stop early enough to set up my books and CDs before people started to arrive. Then she introduced me to some of the local rock stars on their scene: Praises, Robert, and J. E. My eyes were drawn to J. E. He was brown-skinned, with a thin mustache and a devilish smile you could get lost in. I took to him quickly, since he was the comedian of the group. We laughed all night, in the way children do when they're in the classroom and have to use their six-inch voices, but still cause mischief. At the end of the night, we parted ways, but his name couldn't escape my mouth. I spent the car ride to Nee Nee's talking about how cute he was and prying her for answers surrounding his commitment level, availability, and interest in brown-skin girls who were built like brick and mortar, ones who wrote poetry, and maybe lived in another town. No one specific. She laughed me off and gave me a quick city tour as the night became deep and my jet lag set in.

When we arrived at her house, Nee Nee welcomed me into her two-bedroom apartment, a shrine to Africana. I should've guessed by the way her dreads stayed perfectly manicured that her house would smell of incense and Orisha. It was ornately decorated. Most of the pieces were of chameleons in all their nude glory. A bounty of bare bosoms, from sculptures to paintings. A large red couch sat in the center of the living room facing the television. She informed me that I would be taking the back bedroom and I could put my bags down there if I liked. Then another woman emerged.

She was harder in appearance, like a bull bound around the chest. I can't recall her name, because I was so taken aback by how small she felt next to Nee Nee. She wasn't a small woman, but the struggling confidence turned her into a shriveled weed that hid behind her glasses. Nee Nee introduced her as her woman, barely making eye contact and snapping her to her side. They exchanged a kiss, and she quickly disappeared behind the door of the master bedroom. Nee Nee and I talked as her woman floated in and out of the kitchen throughout the night, never lifting her head beyond a nod to Nee Nee almost out of permission; never staying too long to do more than gather water and slip away. Their relationship was odd and uncomfortable, in the way a child who hides their parents' secret is an invisible part of the family. I tried not to pay too much attention to it; instead, I shifted my attention back onto J. E. Finally, Nee Nee agreed to investigate if he was interested. A smile, wide and growing, spread across my face as her woman caught my eyes for a moment. It was a look like she wanted to tell me something but couldn't with Nee Nee present. But I couldn't shake Nee Nee; she was my host, after all. She was offering to house me and feed me for the duration of my stay. Whatever thing was going on with them, I wanted no part of it.

The next day, Nee Nee had to work, so I slept in and chilled around the house until she returned about halfway through the day. Her woman was there, but more ghostlike than there. Floating, haunting, until Nee Nee returned with a more polished and kept woman wrapped around her arm. Nee Nee introduced me to her girlfriend. I am sure my face contorted at this introduction. I had never met anyone in an open relationship. At least, I thought they were open until I looked at the door of the master bedroom where Nee Nee's woman filled the entire frame. The two women who loved her exchanged familiar eye rolls. Nee Nee coughed, and they echoed cordial hellos. The strings around Nee Nee's heart pulled in both directions, but she seemed unmoved. Before any mudslinging could start, Nee Nee cut the tension by announcing that she had invited J. E. over to hang out and put in a good word for me. I was so excited that I ignored the way Nee Nee's partner sat across the couch from her and her girlfriend scowling at their entire existence. I ran to get ready for my next show at a local nightclub that night. Their issues seemed safer when avoided, so I decided to stay in the room until Nee Nee said it was time to leave.

In the waiting time, my manager called me. Our partnership was a new business venture, but I was determined to be a real artist with a manager on top of it. Unfortunately, the person who I picked wasn't as dedicated to finalizing my travel plans as he was to bragging about my talent. And a lapse of judgment caused him to forget to book my flight home. I would be stuck in the Mile High City until the foreseeable future. But when I called Nee Nee into the room to tell her, she took it all in stride. She even offered to use her airline miles to book me on a cheap flight home. I was so grateful to find someone with such a big heart and the willingness to take care of me. And all of it with such ease. By the time I arrived at the club to perform, it was like a weight had been lifted from my shoulders. I felt like I had found family in her, no matter how strange things seemed to be within the walls of her home.

The show went well. Typical fighting for vocal space over intoxicated patrons, peddling CDs and poems, and trying to hear the aspiring poet read me their poem written on the back of a receipt in a dark corner. After a long evening of peopling, I crashed. When I woke up, I stumbled out of my room to find Nee Nee sitting on the floor between her woman's legs, her head cocked to one side while beeswax and coconut oil were married to tighten her dreads. Her partner gave a head nod and continued to pull the hair tighter in silence.

"Tonight is the night! Your boy J. E. is coming over. How are you feeling?"

"I'm good just hanging out, you know, nothing big." I tried to play down my heart thumping.

"You ever slept with a poet before?"

"No. Why?"

"Oh, so you're all innocent and stuff?"

"I mean, I'm just waiting for the right person."

"Well, you aren't getting any younger and you are missing out." She patted her partner on her inner thigh. Her partner looked up at me without cracking a smile. They resumed.

"So you aren't gonna give J. E. none?" she said.

I didn't know. Was this the thing women planned out before the date even arrived? Then I started to feel trapped. I was in her home with three days before my flight and no vehicle to run away. I didn't think she would hurt me. She was just talking, right?

By the time I awakened from my overanalyzing paralysis, the day was now evening and Nee Nee's dreads were glistening in the fluorescent lights. The doorbell rang. It was J. E. He was dapper with a fedora leaning cleanly over one eye. He said hello and greeted me with a hug that smelled like fresh shea butter and aloe. Nee Nee and her women had filled the living room by then. She said he and I could talk in the bedroom. I just wanted to escape whatever was going on between her and these women. We made our way to the back of the house and Nee Nee followed us under the guise of "needing something from a back closet." J. E. went in the room. As I turned to follow, Nee Nee whispered, "It's time to lose your poetry virginity," and shoved me into the bedroom. I reached back to escape, but it was too late. The door was locked from the outside.

I didn't know what she promised J. E., but I didn't put it past her to sell him on the idea of me. I had seen how quickly people could become three-headed. I remembered how quickly Ashley and Michael had shown their scales. I clenched my fists and pressed my back up to the wooden door, ready to fight. He started to call me closer, but I didn't budge. He pulled out a chair and then sat on the bed across from it.

"So, you from the Space City or you just live there?" he asked.

I inched toward the seat, thinking any sudden move would trigger him to switch.

"I'm originally from outside the City of Angels, but I'm based in Space City now." I sat.

Then we talked. He said he just wanted to get to know me. I treaded lightly.

"What got you into poetry?"

I prodded, hoping that my father's truth-conjuring tendencies would prove hereditary with each of his breaths.

"I started years ago, after high school when . . ."

His voice drifted into murmur, one safe and warm. He seemed to have no agenda, falling into soliloquy of childhood, laughing to himself, as my legs tired. My body inched closer, looking for relief from the fighter's stance, and sat at the edge of the bed, still ready to jump back up at any moment. But no threat emerged. My shoulders fell from my ears, and my bricks began to crumble, until I was open enough to scoot up the bed beside him. We talked for over an hour. All of the laughter filled my cheeks, until I could close my eyes without flinching.

By the time Nee Nee returned to see if the deed was done, I had almost forgotten we were trapped in the first place. She unlocked the door, and we got out before she realized the bed was still made. J. E. exchanged numbers with me and promised he would call. Then he pushed by Nee Nee without a word and headed for the front door.

"Well, did you do it?" she asked.

I shook my head in disbelief and made my way past her. I walked J. E. to the door and said good night. When I walked back to the living room, I found Nee Nee sprawled across her woman's lap watching TV. I wanted her to apologize, to acknowledge that she had crossed a line, to know that lines exist even when she blurred them for herself. But she just sat there, with her head in her woman's lap. Like she owned the whole ocean and everything in it. Her woman and I caught eyes; we held a long stare. Like a seasoned prisoner welcoming a new convict into their cell, with both pity and foreboding. Both knowing that a fight with her was too big for either of us to handle. And while we may have wanted to run, both of us knew, as much as we wanted to, there was no way out.

The Hydra bets on some allegiance. Calls Death by her government name, knows things only a sister would. Bends her hand to clean up her mess. Remembers the secrets she sealed behind her lips like a block of ice no one could pick through. The Hydra makes excuses, dismisses accusations, leaves Death holding all the faces, and then asks why she is so anxious. Looks so much like you that you blame yourself.

And Death usually doesn't fight as hard the first round. Most of us come to her young and running from something we perceive to be stronger. I have to admit that I have not always run in the right direction. That I have returned to the den of dragons for the thrill. The way a wolf revisits its vomit, I have believed I could find something nourishing in an already macerated relationship. I own my naivety, be it as it may, but I will not tell you of the final fight you want to hear. Not because it didn't happen, but because breathing words into a thing gives it life. And some things don't need to be resurrected. But I will acknowledge every time that Death gathered me up and threw the match out of grace. So here:

This is the only account of the time the dragon won.
He doesn't get to have history too.

I pray this for grace. It seems to be the only way to move on. Grace with oneself. For what is failure but a chance to learn one's limitations. What is falling down but a chance to rehabilitate your legs? My grandmother believed grace could reimagine any ending. For what is the point of granting grace unless you believe in a person's power? I will show you, the way my grandmother showed me.

Years after reclaiming my time, I sit in the back room of Gma's house, just south of the divine-dotted horizon. I often stop by on my way home from work when the traffic on the 405 becomes a parking lot or I just miss the smell of the potpourri in her untouchable white living room. I make my way down the shotgun hallway with the wall filled with family collages. My mother in college, her sisters and their children, black-and-white, sepia. I make my way past the front bathroom and find her nestled in the small guestroom. The bed sits opposite the blue love seat, next to the recliner that can lift her to a full standing position when she is too weak to do it for herself. A small box TV watches her as she fades in and out of sleep.

I am always getting to know her, the way I am still getting to know myself. Gma doesn't speak of the City of Motors, though I have pieced together that she lived there, like I did. Went to school for business, ate at the casinos in Greektown, and loved the men working the factory line. Maybe she stayed long enough for some kind of dragon to find her, before hunkering down in the City of Angels. We are all kin to fire spitters somehow.

Now when I visit, she lies in bed, Arthur paining her hands and legs. But she is grateful to have life and company. We watch *Flea Market Flip*. We don't mean to watch so many in a row. There is just something about watching the discarded become valuable that we both need to be reminded of. We bet on what piece will go to the highest bidder. I tell her that some things are just too broken to be beautiful again, and she tells me to "give it time" and "keep watching." She falls asleep halfway through and wakes just before the reveal. Though we are at a place beyond talking, she lifts her eyebrows like a million words when the new lacquer is unveiled. As if to say, *See? What did I tell you?* Sometimes we sit in silence for hours, drifting in and out of focus. I have not told her that the dragon found me too. I assume she knows. Recognizes the smell on me. I wonder how long she has known the scent. Neither of us question any of it aloud. She just waits to raise her brows, like she is betting on me every time. Like she can see beyond the rust and singe he left and is just waiting for the big reveal.

I only hope that it is not too late to receive her grace. To learn the lesson before the gods push repeat. For what is a story if you never arrive at the moral? What is a mother, if she never saves you from seeing her same kind of suffering?

The week my daughter's lungs started to develop,
there should've been a giggle resonating across my
abdomen, my baby could finally breathe on her own.

Instead I found myself wondering
How loud would she be able to scream

If someone touched her hands
like chloroform?
Would her voice fire engine?
Would her lungs charge her vocal cords
Would anyone in a five-mile radius feel
lightning strike?

At a familiar candy
An unfamiliar car
would this daughter of mine go willingly?

Would she be able to do
what her mother was unable to?

Decipher in an inhale who to trust?
Know when their scent changes?
Smell the dissolving powder at the
bottom of a glass of alcohol?

To escape? Hold her breath
long enough to tuck and roll
around the 610 loop?

Had I given extra gills on the
inside in case someone tried
to drown her?
To shove her on a ship

in the middle of the Gulf? Could
she respire well enough to make
it back home?

Her kicking fins
not strong enough
for the dangers of silence
a trachea of consequences

Had I shown her how to banshee?
Siren at a grabbing?
To keep herself from becoming
an odyssey? Sustain her pitch long enough
to melt Odysseus's beeswax?

Never give up? When the tide rises?
Load her windpipe like a shotgun
and buckshot when need be?

Living in the South makes her an easier
commodity to traffic
I pray she is learning to landlock her voice,
Build her esophagus into a bell tower
to ring or scream

Woman can be such a foreign
Language of no's

but if she bellows a duodenum
of gong and mallet tongue she can
clang a piercing alarm.

I promise, Momma
will always find you.

So I offer this redemption from Fear. I assure you that denouncing shame is the only way out. To set the things done in the dark into the light and watch them glow. To say, I long to be close even though my body winces at the touch. To still want the touch despite it. To offer my body a living sacrifice. To let someone behind the veil of my holy tapestry. I will tell you there is a reclamation in that. One we often demoralize by frequency. But what power hides in the breaking of bodies? The taking and eating. Let us not forget what power comes when we are down on our knees.

It is not about the times I loved you
but the times I hated me
Enough to stay.

Love and the Southern Behemoth

No one speaks of the Red Mountain anymore. They spend all day analyzing Silurian rock strata, the Sloss Mines, and quartz pebbles that wash up when the tide rolls in. No one tells the story of how it got red in the first place.

Love has always been a provider. She once roamed the earth in sandstone skin, stood taller than the alder trees. Bunyan had nothing on the way she shaped every hill the South holds sacred. Her broad shoulders and proud chest cocked her twenty-foot cast-iron sledgehammer back to pummel her sharpened chisel, until the earth fell away and all that was left standing was majesty and muscle and mountain. Her callused hands dragged the hilt of that Southern Behemoth down through the clay bed till the groundwater broke into river mouth and ran the Cahaba all the way down to the river basin. And when the silt was settling and the cardinals were making their nests, the sound of her fashioning mound or metal into magnificence echoed a steady clink that gave the day a measure of seconds and minutes. Some say she created time itself. Or at least its constructs. Love's giant furnace used to roar and rumble all day. She would mine iron by the handful to keep the blazing fire—which offered light to the day and heat to the night for the nearby Emberlungs—alive.

They were a small village of people. Free by some act of running. Saved by Love's hands. The Emberlungs came to her by happenstance. Followed the Drinking Gourd till the exhaustion turned the stars into kaleidoscope. Celestial bodies shifting in dizzy rhythm. She wasn't looking for anything but a new place to sculpt something beautiful, when she stumbled upon their unconscious bodies. They were so tiny that, all together, they barely filled her palms. And for some reason, she took a liking to them. Maybe it was the sparks, the pinpricks of light moving in their own orbit across the chests of the determined people that told her they were special, that made her seek to keep them alive long enough to see them grow to full flame. She crafted them a home deep in the side of the hill just beyond her furnace; that way, if someone came looking, they would have to pass her and the Southern Behemoth to steal them back. And the Emberlungs lived there, at the back of Love's furnace, for years before anyone ever tried to come for them. They used the stones at the lips of the river to scrub their clothes clean. They harvested pecans from nearby trees and made offerings of warm pies during the season dedicated to Love. They helped her name each range and sculpture in ways Adam only knew. And when Love was low on inspiration, they sang praises of the things she had done, the ways she moved the earth just for them, all keyed to the rhythm of the descending hammer. The Emberlungs, these friends to Love, did all this of their own volition. Coming and going the same way as the fish and the wind. And Love would've had it no other way, but she did have some rules.

In order to keep the Emberlungs safe, Love offered some agreements to guide their living under her hearth. First, they must always feed their lights, the parts of them that knew better was always on the horizon and that they were deserving of space in every timeline. They must find a way to keep that spirit alive at all costs. Second, the Emberlungs must always be honest with Love. She may not like what they had to say, but Love would always listen and help them find a way to traverse any trouble that came their way. And third, they must always keep the furnace burning. As long as the fire burned blue, there would be no smoke. This would keep any hunters from finding the Emberlungs and snatching them from Love's grasp. And these were the only governing rules. In all else, the Emberlungs had their freedom.

Love spent long days flattening sections of land into rolling plains or carving the Gulf with her knuckles, while the Emberlungs played, laughed, and tended to her furnace.

As the sun retired to rest, Love would take her place by the furnace to listen to the tiny voices sing the sweetest lullaby and lull her to sleep. At first, all things worked in harmony, the Emberlungs multiplying in number as the hum of their songs joined the predictable pound of Love's relentless work in a romantic swoon that made the birds envy them. But over time, the monotony of fire labor lost its luster, and soon the Emberlungs started to forget the captivity from which they came, replacing it with complaints of where they were. There was no greater complainer than Ronald Emberlung.

Ronald was a small but strong man. He used to help fit horseshoes for Acirema's servants. His position close to the ground made the work easy, and he was all about easy work. He never expected that his two daughters and wife would disappear into the trees right before his eyes. He had little left to live for with them gone and no more allegiance to Acirema, so he ran. He made the choice that living without them was hell and he was ready for a free Heaven. His stout, muscle-bound legs made the run a true dedication. So when he woke in Love's hand, months before reaching northern light, he was grateful to find an easier path to safety. But he wasn't prepared to live under Love's rule.

His grateful heart was the first to turn cold. But all you need is one fading spark, and the ashes come. He would take his shifts at the fire begrudgingly, tossing too little coal into the fire, cooling it until peaks of smoke would start to lift just past the canopy. His fellow Emberlung workers would try to pick up his slack, as he spent hours complaining about Love's harsh rule, as if he had known none harsher. Day after day they went on listening to his bitter criticism.

"Why we gotta keep this flame high? Y'all see how big she is? She could toss a heap of coal in a single handful that would keep this fire cobalt for centuries. She don't need us, only wants us to suffer in the shadow of her dirty work. And what was she doing before we came? She surely had a fire without us. She is just another captor trying to bleed us for all we got. Are y'all just gonna go along with it?"

At first his questioning was a seed on stony ground, taking no root, but soon ears started to soften. Before long, more and more Emberlungs ruminated on his questioning and had questions of their own.

One woman asked, "I wonder why Love needs all of this heat in the summer months. I mean, can't she just dip her chisel into the sun? She's close enough."

Another man reasoned, "How long does she expect us to callus our hands with this work? When do we get to be the ones taken care of?"

Others found ways to complain about petty things: the volume of her laugh, being tired of singing, her ravenous appetite for all the pecan pies that left nothing for the Emberlungs who made them. And the seed of discontent grew roots. Then, one day, Ronald Emberlung decided to take a stand.

"We should just stop feeding the fire. Let it go to ash

and then see if she appreciates all that we do around here for Love."

He had the people's ear, and the sparks in their chests began to dim. They agreed to take action the next day while Love was away but until then to pretend everything was normal.

The night before the revolution, she stumbled home after a long day spent putting the finishing touches on a special mountain. This one, a new home for the Emberlungs, took months for Love to prepare. She shaped it to provide protection on every side, with valleys and winding trails meticulously carved with precision. They would no longer need to tend the fire with such rigor, because Love could spread them far and wide without worrying of any danger. She planned to unveil it to them the next day under the setting sun, but when she returned home something was off. She watched as the Emberlungs moved in a predictable fashion. They beat their clothes, served their pies, and sang their songs, but their hearts didn't seem to be in it. In fact, on closer examination, there were few chest embers to be counted among the lot. Love called a town meeting, begging them to tell her if something was wrong or if they needed anything. But true to plan, Ronald and the others remained quiet and assured Love that the missing light was just their need for rest. And while she didn't believe them, she held on to hope that their truth would finally show itself, the way the Emberlungs promised her it would.

But promises to Love are bought at a dime a million. And once she fell asleep, they gathered to give final orders. When Love left the next day, they would stop feeding the fire. Slowly the azure flame would simmer to red and then to a gray soot that would signal for miles their stance against Love. Ronald would give the signal, of course. The night shift fed the hungry blaze through the night and part of the morning. As Love rose to leave, she asked one more time if everything was all right and was assured things were fine.

Steps away, she put her final touches on the new village. She replanted trees and even strung a rope swing, hand-braided from her discarded hair and driftwood from the Gulf, for the youngest Emberlungs to swing on. She built little homes and placed them just far enough away from each other that an ask for sugar was still plausible, but that sound remained their own. She was just getting ready for the grand reveal when she noticed the smoke. The small black snake of cinder slithering into a cloud that reached from one village to the next. She stopped everything she was doing and made her way as quickly as she could, without destroying any forests, back to camp.

When she arrived, the Emberlungs formed a wall with their bodies in front of the furnace. Ronald stood in front of them, ready with a written statement of complaint. Love bent down to them, trying to get to the furnace without injuring them, but they clawed and bit at her hand until she pulled back in pain. Then Ronald pulled out a bullhorn and spoke loudly to Love's ears.

"We are tired of doing your dirty work. You spend days by the beach and in the mountains, relaxing among the tallest trees while we toil away under the heat of your fire. But all that ends today. We were strong enough to find our way here. We are strong enough to keep ourselves safe without you."

The people's tiny murmurs turned to cheers. And as soon as the last word fell from Ronald's mouth, he and Love knew just how big a mistake it all was. The hunters had arrived. They came in droves when they saw the smoke. They knew a cloud that big could only be made by a large group of runners and would provide a hefty ransom once returned. Love had no time to be hurt or try to reason. The Emberlungs were facing a new trouble, and only one thing could stop them.

Love was scared that if she just picked everyone up and ran, they would be too easy to track. This time, the Emberlungs would have to help. The horde of hunters was now an exploding ant mound of men, firing guns and lassoing bodies like they sought to feast. Love pointed groups of Emberlungs to different trails; she knew their new homes would keep them safe if she could just get them there. They ran in packs as Love tried to keep the hunters pinned near the cooling furnace. She was able to toss some of them in the smoldering ash; others crawled up her arms into her hair.

They tried to bite, claw, and tear at her skin with all their might, but Love was able to keep them busy long enough for most of the Emberlungs to disappear into the mountains, including Ronald.

When the roads merged, the fleeing survivors found themselves looking down on Love's gift. They saw the houses and the swing, the tiny roads and all the high valley walls made for keeping things out, like a giant moat around a castle. Instantly their stomachs were filled with guilt. Behind them, Love was laying everything on the line to keep them safe, and before them, proved she always had.

Ronald spoke up. "Let's run to the houses and lock ourselves in. If we keep all the lights off, no one will even know we are in there."

But the smallest Emberlung, Vi, had a different suggestion. She was almost as tall as Ronald, but decades younger, a chest of fluttering light. Her taut puffs balanced on each side of her head as she climbed up a nearby tree whose branch looked sturdy enough to hold her. She sat above the remaining Emberlungs as those divided by regret and panic looked for a quick fix to this mess they had made. Vi clapped her hands until she had everyone's attention.

"Are we just going to let them kill her? Love is the only reason we have made it this far. My mother has told me the story of how Love found her while I was still in her belly. She is the only reason I am alive today. She has provided us with food and shelter and safety and this is how we will repay her?"

Many of the Emberlungs hung their heads in shame. Some mumbled to themselves, while others looked back to see if they could spot Love's body grunting under the weight of the multiplying hunters. Ronald tried to speak up again but was quickly quieted by Vi's growing confidence.

"Enough complaining! That's how we got here in the first place. And now before us sits this mountain, this gift made by Love—are we to take it and leave her behind? It's time we fought for Love as hard as she has fought for us!"

Then light crawled, the way it does when a door is slowly opening after a long night, across each Emberlung's chest. Vi had stirred something deep inside them that was almost forgotten, almost extinguished entirely. And the Emberlungs were alight and determined, like the first night they ran into Love's arms. All but Ronald of course. He sat grumbling as everyone else took to the mountain to join hands in song.

Love now lay there, a body infested with hunters who had tied her up with rope. She gasped for air as their tiny bodies worked together to take over the Southern Behemoth and move it toward Love's head. She wrestled against the tearing twine, trying to inch a finger or knuckle free, knowing the damage even that could do. But all her tussling was interrupted when she heard the sound. That sweet sound coming down from the hills first mimicked a whistle and grew into a chorus in a matter of seconds. Vi, holding the bullhorn before them and everyone pushing every note from their full diaphragms. "Here we are, Here we are," they sang.

The hunters heard them and quickly dropped all efforts to restrain Love for the purse of the capture. The hunters took toward the hills, scattering in and out and through toward the rising song, "Here we are, Here we are."

And then Love was still. She held back her tears for fear of flooding the plains. She wriggled and writhed until she was free. Her mind set on making things right. She grabbed the mighty Behemoth and headed for the hill.

She arrived just as the hunters cleared the valley. Each Emberlung took a knee on the hillside, as their song added meaning: "Here We Are, Here We Are Love, Ready for Your Strike."

She looked at the hunters scurrying closer and closer. She looked at the people, hearts of pure light. She thought of all they had run from, how tired they lay in her hands on the first night, how desperate they were to live life on their own terms. So desperate in fact that they rebelled against even her hand. Love looked at the Behemoth. She looked into their ready hearts. Then she knew. She cocked it back with all her might and let the hammer descend upon the hill with a mighty blow that ignited every chest into full flame and turned the mountain volcanic.

Their blood ran down every path, lava on every side, until it settled so deep into the clay, it could not be scrubbed out. Love stared at the ground until it ceased to move—not Vi or Ronald or any hunter seemed to remain. Every Emberlung was lost to the mighty strike. Love sat there heartbroken, long enough for the birds to recover from the resound and return to nesting in nearby treetops. And in Love's final act, she buried her hammer there as a monument to them. She gathered all she could of the Emberlungs and the earth and stacked it as high as she could muster, until it enveloped her hammer and sat as close to Heaven as she could manage.

For greater friend hath no one than this, than those who lay their lives down for Love.

Fairy Dust and Legends

There is no point in denoting a first path to Death if there isn't a second. This, a less beaten trail, but still viable nonetheless. If the first was force, the second must be attributed to omission. For a story is made equally of the things it chooses to recount and the things it chooses to forget.

The room undulated with the bass of Ray Charles's voice and a choir of laughter. I remember sailing through the bottom half of a dozen black ball gowns as I stood on my father's feet. He held my hands, dipped my eight-year-old body back until my eyes landed on the upside-down image of my grandparents kissing. The gold and white tinsel danced behind them, a hallelujah chorus as fifty years wrapped pulse between their fingers and palms: this was Love.

Growing up, no one had to teach me the value of her.

I saw it every day between my mother and my father, a forty-four-year journey underway, and my grandparents, who counted fifty-eight years before my grandfather lost his final battle with Death. They married young, just before he left to fight in World War II. Just in time to knock her up and leave her to raise my father on her own for the first few years. But that was how it worked in those days. Women were reared to raise a family, bake lemon meringue pies fresh on Father's Day, keep the house. She told me once that she was planning on leaving him. She said the day she darned all his socks and got rid of all the newspapers she was going to be done.

Within seconds of pulling the last stitch tight on that day's pile of damaged socks, my grandfather entered with a haul of outdated papers and slammed them down on the table. He then kissed her and walked upstairs. She stared at the tower of print until she heard her name resounding from the second floor:

GENEVA!!! I NEED YOU TO FIX MY SOCKS!

She looked at us, rolled her eyes, and said, "See what I mean?"

And that was them. He was a rolling thunder that screamed, "Good morning, world!" out of his bedroom to the entire City of Angels every morning before the sun rose. She was a peaceful tide, demure, gliding her hands across your hands across the keys of the organ with grace. She served him like a fifties sitcom wife. They were the honeymooners you couldn't stop watching, even when you wanted to. My grandfather, after all, was a Word Assassin. In one breath he could be in full cackle, and in the next he could be pulling a pin on an f-bomb.

They slept in separate beds in separate rooms. She said it was because he refused to clip his toenails and she was tired of being sliced. I think there was only so much coming home the army left him with. He was a green-eyed, dagger-spitting hothead. My father said he grew up watching his father taunt his mother about her weight and affinity for baked goods. The toll of losing two sets of twins, birthing two children, adopting two others, and that never-leaving loneliness had worn on her body in ways he would never understand. Food was comforting. It was warm and constant and kind. He was brash, and unrelenting, and when he would lay into her, she crumbled. He would find some way to fit her weight or her ineptitude in as the butt of every joke. And most days she would let it all slide, standing to grab the laundry or make his plate with a hidden flex of mouth or crumpled nose, exiting without a word.

She loved him. I don't doubt that. We saw it every New Year's Eve when she would tuck the grands in her bed and sneak off to his. They would lie together as the new year and another year of matrimony converged. In the morning, we would wake before the sun, watch him carry two two-by-fours and a metal ladder down Orange Boulevard to watch the Parade of Roses live. She would saunter behind him, trying to adjust the strap on the canteen full of hot chocolate, or the blankets, or the lunch sacks, or to grab the flighty children's hands, and he would yell that she was "too slow" and "holding him up." She would tell him to "shut up" sometimes, but mostly she would just roll her eyes and wait for the times that his sweetness overwhelmed her heart again. Marriage isn't about swooning every moment; it's about holding on through the times you absolutely hate them, in the faith that you can love them again.

I see so much of her in my father and so much of my father in me. My grandfather always knew how to love me close enough to prick. He would offer to sneak me candy when my mom wasn't looking, then cuss me out for not being able to get it open quietly. He was such a seesaw. And we rode every high.

When I was five, he told me to fill up the bathtub to get clean. I told him I didn't know how. He was short with me. Said it was "just filling up the tub with water." So I walked over the black-and-white checkered floor where the heat didn't hit. I plugged the tub with the rubber stopper and turned one of the handles. The water rushed in quickly. I stripped down to nothing and dangled my feet into the tub when it was half full, only to find the water was a frigid sea. I wrapped myself in a towel and went to tell him. He began to yell. The next thing I knew, he was storming past me, racing toward the tub.

He dipped his hand in and pulled it back like he had frostbite.

"WHY WOULD YOU FILL THE TUB WITH COLD WATER?"

"I told you I—"

"WHY WOULD YOU FILL THE MOTHAFUCKING TUB LIKE THIS?

"DON'T YOU KNOW HOW MUCH MONEY THIS SHIT IS?"

My grandmother stood petrified behind him for a moment before throwing her body between us.

"CARL, SHE'S JUST A CHILD! LEAVE HER ALONE!"

She wasn't shocked at the way he spoke, just that he had forgotten his manners with a child. She snatched me and took me to sit by the fire my grandfather burned all year long in every season. She held me close to her chest and rubbed her soft hands over my arms and shoulders until I was warm.

In a moment's time, he came back hungry. He sat in the chair closest to me watching *60 Minutes* and asked me if I wanted to join him. She brought him the floral TV tray and kissed him on the forehead. Then she called me close to her and taught me how to rerun the bathwater for the next time. There were no apologies. I guess when you love this long, you don't waste time saying you're sorry.

I guess all love requires a bit of death. What are Love and Death but star-crossed lovers anyhow? Ask any of our mothers that. They have all lost track of themselves one time or another. And I am no exception. We have all made ourselves a mustard seed in a lover's potential. Risked who we were for who we could be with someone else. But the greatest crime was not in taking the risk but in forgetting who we were after we rolled the dice.

He was fine. Blaxican with the pretty eyes y skin made from Ibarra. The only man to roll the *r* in my name. Second lunch. We were worlds apart in the quad. The football players and popular girls ran the main girth, JROTC took the hill, the most attractive guys snuck girls into the theater to practice being grown. I hung somewhere between the nerds who would probably run every Fortune 500 tech company started by a millennial and the outcasts who sprawled at the base of the Empire's lowest mountain in pairs. He was transient. Making his way between every world. He and his two cousins. Carbon-copy lucha libres that flanked him on either side. Big boys with mild skin. He was charismatic; they were intimidating. I never minded them much 'cause the way we caught eyes during the break said it was only a matter of time before . . .

My male friends teased that I was a late bloomer. I had never kissed a boy before. But this was high school, and the sun was high. And there was something about the way he licked his lips. I don't remember when we got together. Just the moment we stood under the cement arch and he bent my body into him. His hand in the small of my back. His thumb against my chin. Time stood still. My mouth, no longer virgin or unknown. The silence, all but his warm fifteen-year-aged breath. Sun-kissed. He was experienced enough to walk away. That saunter that knew he was wanted and begged me to chase him. And I did. All the way across the quad. To that back corner where the cameras went blind. And his cousins took watch of any rogue security guards looking for a way to unhook our mouths. Then the bell would ring, and they would disappear. Three goons into the night. The way a bad boy does and a good girl watches.

And I watched him every day after school. Catch and release. He would swim against the current of fleeing students and then just disappear. I would hold his breath in my mouth till I couldn't see him anymore. Almost fainted when second semester put him in my gym class. There is something about a boy glistening with his own sweat that beckons. He gave me the fastest mile I ever ran. He would strip to skins to play basketball. I can't remember if he was any good, but I saw every game, in slow motion. He would rub his slick, brown chest against my back on his way to the locker rooms. I would pretend like I didn't see him. Then we would smile. Wait for the bell like Cupid waits for his arrows to prick. Hungry, I tried to find him earlier, but he was never an easy one to catch. I baited him with love notes. When he didn't come, I remembered my play brothers cracking jokes near the vending machines. They asked me where I had been. I told them handling my business. They didn't pry.

Then I saw him on the hill. Cousin on either side. I waved. He swam away. The way a shark does when you hook it in the snout and it swims so far out it tears your entire reel from your hands.

I figured he just didn't see me. Till after school. From out of nowhere, four hands, mild and squeezing tighter, thrust me up against the stucco wall, back there where the cameras' eyes were plucked. He stood beneath me, hot as Abuelita cocoa, as his cousins pinned me high on the wall. Wanting to know who those boys were I was with before third period. I stuttered. He asked if I thought he was blind. Grabbed me by the chin and made me look him in the eyes. I swore it wasn't what it looked like. He told me it better not be, then they dropped me. I hit the concrete with enough force to send pain radiating through each shin. I watched him break my hook and swim away.

I spent the rest of the day brushing off the dust, checking all the bruises that were too early to see darkening under my skin. When it came time to return to class, I bought a Powerade from the vending machine that always gave you two and told the teacher it was that time of the month so he wouldn't make me run. Then I sat just close enough to see what I thought was his brown body swirl through the key of the court. Before I could see if the ball went in, he was sliding behind me, leg on either side, kissing an apology into my neck. He never said it, but I knew he was overreacting. He bashfully pushed his nose to my cheek and then his lips to mine. Warmer than before. I melted in his lap. Then he took me by the hand and led me closer. Kissed his fingers into a peace sign and winked. I cracked the seal on the bottle and exhaled into the next week, where the bell rang like it always did, but this time he waited for me outside the locker room.

It was supposed to rain that day and he wanted to walk me to lunch. His cousins were trailing us by the time we passed where the Domino's pizzas and chimichangas were sold. I told him I had to turn something in for French class. He told me I could do it later. I said it was already late and tried to walk away. Then their hands again. Grabbed me and twisted my arms backward for him. His knuckle sliding against my cheek. He told me I was staying. Asked me, didn't I want to? I did but . . . Then he kissed me. Mid-explanation. Held me so close I couldn't breathe. When the bell rang, I ran to French class and turned in my paper behind the teacher's back. Snuck out and sprinted all the way to the locker room. The black clouds swarming over spring. The patter of drops driving behind me. I slipped in the aluminum doors just in time to get on my kelly greens and white tee and line up on the baseline.

When the weather was bad, all the gym teachers would bring their classes inside and we would run the mile around the basketball court in shifts. Boys first, then girls. He was midsprint when I finally tracked him with my eyes. He blew me a kiss. I caught it. The second time around, a friend of mine decided to roll his eyelids back and scare the girls beside me. They screamed. I laughed. Too hard I guess. Before the giggle could finish falling from my mouth, I felt a prick. A stabbing throb against my throat. I looked up only to see him, Malecko, his face stony and disapproving. Beneath me, an open safety pin dislodged from my neck and hit the floor.

When it was my turn to run, I didn't stop at the baseline or the bleachers or where the cameras refused to look. I ran right into after school. I wanted to write it off as an accident or as the things that women built like me would have to settle for to be loved. By then, I was a boat home at best. A floating reminder of how my appetite deceived my body, how my hormones were waiting on me to get it all together. I should've been happy he swam my way in the first place. I waited around hoping to catch him before he was out the gates. I followed the parting sea only to find him. Thumb in back pockets. Chest pressed against hers. Tongue fishing-lined down her throat. Caught.

I don't know who told the story first. The one that says Love is supposed to sweep you off your feet, but it wasn't Love. No, she is much more sure-footed. Maybe it was Death. She has always been a hopeless romantic. Still, Love only comes when your mind and your heart are in covenant. The rest is just fairy dust and legends. But we have long lost our desire for anything but falling. We fancy the forbidden. We barter with our own instinct for a tiny moment of fancy. And in all of it, we forget that our mothers have done this before. What selfish ways we choose Death over Love.

Boo Boo and Her Little Friend

A long time ago, before our mothers were old enough to test the boundaries, her name was already a rumor told on porch steps and kitchen fights. Her mother named her Bonita. She held that name until she was old enough to meet a man fine enough to change it to Boo Boo. Shaped like a pear from an early age, Boo Boo learned young, like we all have, that a good man is worth catching no matter how fast he runs. She got a reputation early of being the kind of girl who gives herself away often. But it is written, every social outcast is allotted one best friend. An equally atrocious accomplice. And for Boo Boo, Gertie's daughter, Her Little Friend, was just that.

Her Little Friend came with her own baggage. A father who denied her and a mother with five other children on either side of her, often left her to fend for herself. They stumbled upon each other one day while walking home from the bus stop after school. Her Little Friend noticed Boo Boo's backpack was open. Probably an older kid's foiled prank to drop lit Black Cats in her bag when she wasn't looking. But Her Little Friend saw it as an opportunity to reach out. She flagged her down at the corner and helped her unstick the overused zipper. And just like that a friendship was born. They grew into their hips around eighth grade, two inverted question marks sauntering into high school. Then college. Somehow still thick as thieves after all these years. They would alternate Saturday-morning brunches at each other's apartments near campus. They would spend late nights dishing gossip and making vision boards on the loves of their lives. Channing Tatum types. Michael B. Jordans dressed in everyday. Then entered Brian.

He was an out-of-state student who had taken a gap year to help his father bury his mother. He wasn't the model type. More of a bamboo child, every day growing bigger and more developed than the next. But there was something in him that Boo Boo found intriguing. Potential, maybe. Her Little Friend, like any good wingwoman, asked around if he was attached to anyone's heart. Most people didn't know who she was speaking of. If they did, they knew nothing about his romantic life. Boo Boo knew the only way to play this was to get to know him better. Her Little Friend knew exactly how to make this happen.

"Let's throw a kickback. We can have music and play spades. Keep it low stakes. I bet you can get his attention."

But the night of the party didn't go entirely as planned. Boo Boo and Her Little Friend ended up playing opposite Brian and his friend Daryl in a game of spades. As they rounded the final hand, the girls held a considerable lead. Her Little Friend, always a boaster, convinced Brian and Daryl that proof of their manhood was tied to winning. Taunting, she persuaded them to go blind and bid big. After a crushing loss, Brian and Daryl wanted nothing to do with celebrating. They made their quick exit shortly after.

Her Little Friend suggested giving him his space.

"You ain't want no man that can't celebrate your win anyway, Sis!"

Boo Boo heard her but felt crushed until she bumped into Brian at the student union. He had on a fleece hoodie and a nice pair of Timbs. His jeans hugged his growing thighs, and he seemed to take up more air than before. Brian didn't budge when he saw Boo Boo headed in his direction. He thanked her for a great night and apologized for leaving like that. She forgave him, and he asked her to grab lunch together. Boo Boo felt that pulse-igniting love mushrooming in her chest. She knew how dangerous it could be. She tried to keep her emotions in check, but by the end of the week, secret pictures she had taken of Brian were making their way onto her vision board.

The next week, Boo Boo took an early bus to campus to study before a test. It dropped her off near the library, farther away from her eight a.m. class. She spotted Brian near the quad talking up Daryl. He waved her down and asked her to have lunch with him. She blushed so hard and long that she lost focus for her entire three-hour lecture. By the time lunch came, she had convinced herself that this would be the time to tell Brian how she felt. They met at the union near the food court. Before Boo Boo could say a word, Brian asked her for some advice. She was humbled that he would ask her.

"So I know we haven't really known each other for long, but I feel like you get me."

Boo Boo nodded.

"You know I'm not super public about my love life, but, uh . . . I met somebody and I don't know what to do."

Now convinced that Brian was speaking in code, she readied herself for that movie moment when he revealed that she was all he ever dreamed of and needed. The same feeling that had been pulsing through her hands since that first night.

"Her name is Becky. She's an upperclassman. I just lose myself around her. You're always so good at expressing yourself. I figured you could give me some advice on what to do."

He seemed to overgrow her. Now he was a chute protruding from her clavicle. She couldn't breathe. He could see it. His face started to contort with worry. She excused herself, saying she had forgotten to meet with her professor for office hours. Then she ran and hid in the handicap stall of the union bathroom. Her fingers trembling over the phone as she called Her Little Friend to vent. Like any good friend, Her Little Friend told her what she needed to hear.

"Oblivious Brian just don't know what he's missing. You just got to show him, Boo."

The two had learned from their mothers that when a man doesn't want you, it's your job to show him how many ways he's wrong. The two spent the next hour conspiring about ways to prove Boo Boo's sex appeal and compatibility. In the following weeks, Boo Boo tried everything to get his attention. When long nights with Becky almost made him miss his presentations, Boo Boo showed up with home-made peanut butter fudge cookies, just for him. He sat in the stillness of prayer, no doubt thanking God for Boo Boo, before savoring every morsel. He would look deep into her eyes and then remind her that she was the best friend he could have. When Becky refused to wear matching outfits to homecoming, Boo campaigned throughout the school to get them on the ballot for the "cutest couple that never was." Which, of course, Brian brushed off. When Becky wouldn't get matching tattoos on spring break, Boo Boo invited him to the talent show and sang his favorite song directly to him. He later boasted that only a sister could know how to cheer him up this well. She was appalled. *No one wants to date their sister.* She had to find a way to shake out of the friend zone and quickly, and Her Little Friend had the perfect idea.

"Have you tried a root?"

"Huh?"

"You know, a love spell? One he can't resist. Your momma ain't teach you?"

"No. Tell me."

"You know when the moon wanes and Auntie Flo turns your insides to a magic river? You have to tap your own cur-rent. Bottle it. Then you invite him over for dinner. You set out nice plates, pretty glasses. You make the house full of red flower petals and the juice that looks like merlot. Make yourself up a big pot of pasta. Marinara or vodka sauce.

Then you take that bottle and stir in a little of your magic. Now, be careful. Don't put too much. When he eats it, the love will take root. Girl, he won't be able to leave you without pulling up his entire life."

Boo Boo's eyes swelled large with intrigue. "Say less. Are you sure it will work?"

"Worked for my momma. My daddy couldn't leave if the hunger tried to take him."

Boo Boo had been desperate, but this gave her hope. So she waited for the moon to wane three times over. She filled a small mason jar with her womb elixir and kept it in the bottom of the chest that sat at the foot of her bed. The next time he and his girlfriend got into a fight, she asked Brian over. Told him she just wanted to offer a shoulder. She offered to cook him dinner. Watch Netflix. Chill. He seemed open. Then Boo Boo went to work. To offset the smell, she filled the house with scented candles. Red. She warmed bread smothered in garlic and toasted it on the top rack of the oven. She pulled her gumbo pot from the back of the cabinet and began boiling water. Then she got the jar. Once the noodles had gone limp to the heat, she drained off the excess water and poured in half of the sauce. Then a little magic. She remembered Her Little Friend's warning: "Not too much." But Boo Boo had been patient. She had tried everything with Brian. When else would she have him all to herself? What if she didn't put in enough and it didn't work? This may be her only chance. She poured in the remainder of the mason jar, stirring the rest of the sauce behind it until the two were inseparable.

When Brian arrived, he was so upset that he didn't even notice the ambience. The candles. The soft music. The low lights. He plopped down at the table and began word vomiting all the ways his girlfriend didn't listen. How angry she made him. How he wasn't himself with her. How he didn't feel in control. Boo Boo listened intently while scooping heaps of pasta onto a wide-mouth plate. She put one hand on his back and the plate on the table in front of him. Brian, so irate he didn't even say grace, twisted his fork in circles, wrapping the long dripping noodles around and between the tines. Then he put the first large heap into his mouth. He slurped the long strands into a red pouch circled by his lips. Boo Boo watched anxiously. She hadn't tasted it before giving it to Brian, and she feared her magic would be detectable. And it was.

"Mmmm . . . what is this sauce?" Licking his lips: "I haven't tasted anything like this, you really put your foot in it."

Not quite a foot. Boo Boo snickered to herself. Then she sat near Brian to continue listening to his rant. He went on. With every bite, he seemed to open up more. By the end of his plate, he had decided that staying with his girlfriend was a waste of his passion. She wasn't even worth it. He admitted he should find a woman more like Boo Boo. A good woman. Loyal. Who could cook. So when he asked Boo Boo for seconds, she was happy to oblige. And when he asked for extra bread to sop the plate clean, she brought him an end piece. He ate and drank until he was too full to drive, so Boo Boo offered the couch. Brian settled into the soft brown pillows, cocking his feet up on her ottoman and unbuttoning his pants. She sat next to him and turned on the television. Brian snuggled up to her chest and fell asleep. Boo Boo was surprised how instantaneous the results were. She treasured every breath while holding him close.

The next morning, Boo Boo woke early to make a big, lush breakfast for both of them. She was starving after missing dinner the previous night. She made grits, cheesy and sweet, fried eggs, fresh-squeezed orange juice, and even baked fresh, gooey monkey bread. She set it out in a large buffet on the dining room table. Brian woke to the waft of fresh melted cinnamon sugar. He stumbled over to the table and stared at the elaborate spread. He snuck up and wrapped his arms around Boo Boo's stomach. He thanked God for her. Then he kissed her neck and pulled out her chair. Boo Boo had never seen this side of Brian before. She loved seeing him flirt from across the table as he melted with every nibble. When the meal was done, Boo Boo cleaned the table and Brian took his spot back on the couch. Then Boo Boo went to get dressed for class. She felt a new kind of power, this thing that rose in her at being loved by him. It was like redwood finally breaking the canopy and seeing the sky. Even the air smelled different in Brian's gaze. She took a bodycon dress that she had been scared to wear out of the back of the closet. She put it on and smoothed the creases against her body. She grabbed her bag, ready to take on the new day, and strutted her new confidence through the living room to say goodbye before heading out. Brian looked her up and down like he was seeing her trunk brand-new.

"Where do you think you're going?"

At first Boo Boo took it as jest, but the harshness of Brian's face was one she had only seen when his girlfriend refused to say goodbye in the morning before class.

"Don't nobody need to be seeing all your curves. Those belong to me."

He stood and cupped his hands around her hips.

"Why don't you go on in there and change into something more appropriate for class."

Boo Boo didn't know what to say. She had never been anybody's before. So she went into the room and changed into some jeans and a faded hoodie.

"That's better."

Brian smiled as he tracked her across the room with his eyes. Boo Boo got her book bag and headed for her morning class. On her way, she called Her Little Friend to brag and confirm that it worked.

"Sis, it worked so well, he even picked my clothes out this morning. Is he supposed to be this into me?"

"What, you don't want him to be passionate about what's his?"

"I mean I do, but . . ."

"Don't you want him to want you all to himself?" Her Little Friend questioned.

"Well, yes, but . . ."

"Then you have to submit to what he says. Compromise, Boo."

Boo Boo held a reservation in her gut like a stone that wouldn't pass. But she wrote it off to the naivety of her lack of experience. She went about the day, trying not to think about the dress or the being his—all of it just made her head swim.

But that day when she came home, things looked different. Brian had moved his entire apartment in. His Jordan collection hijacked the door, jerseys filled the closet till overflowing, and he had rerouted her entire TV setup so he could play his Xbox in HD. Then there was Brian, now so comfortable that he sat in the middle of the couch in his boxers and headset playing *Call of Duty*. He looked like he had been there for hours.

Beer cans littered the coffee table and papers with loose weed crumbled across her magazines.

"Brian! What is all of this?"

"Oh, I was just making myself more at home in my baby's place."

He smiled and kissed her on the cheek, his breath still hot as the day was long.

"Can we clean some of this up?" Boo mumbled with an attitude as she slid the cans to one side with the back of her hand, accidentally knocking an open one into Brian's lap.

Brian screamed and tossed down his headset. Boo Boo rushed to grab some towels and clean up the mess before it soaked into her microsuede upholstery, but he caught her before she could clear the love seat.

"Are you trying to ruin my game?" Brian prodded before hovering over Boo Boo's head. "Do you know how long it took me to get to that level?"

Brian knocked the coffee table over in one fell swoop. Then he took the cushions that Boo Boo was right in the middle of cleaning and threw them into the kitchen.

"Are you listening to me?!"

Boo Boo trembled as Brian grabbed her arm and pulled her up to his chest.

"Why you pushing me to this?"

When Brian saw the fear growing in her face, he unpinched her forearm and forced a kiss. Boo Boo recoiled. Then he sat on the floor and resumed his game. Boo Boo tried to back out of the room. She didn't know what to do. Should she kick him out? Could she love him out of it? Just when she made the choice that maybe she needed some space to decide, Brian remarked, "Oh, and I finished off the leftovers from last night. You keep cooking like that, and I'll never leave."

We want what we want when we want it. We forget that everything has its consequence, even life. That religion can be wielded wrong. That our hearts are the most fallow of grounds. I have learned that Fate has its own tenants. But in the end, bending Love to our own measurements never quite fits. And Demise, though waiting with a gentle hand, waits for us still. To remind us what we are worth. Even if we wanted something out of our reach. It is we that hallucinate that all we see before us is familiar enough to call it Love. Oh, how we confuse finding Love with capturing chaos. This, Love's curse. That she makes us see the future. Live in too many timelines for our own good. Treasure hunt with our heart and hold close to everything that sparks. I want to know how to draw a clean line. To be more like Death. To know when to cut the cord. To forgive but remember. But I haven't found a way to stop fighting for the things that seek to take my life. Maybe that too is our burden.

There is a version where I forgive him. We marry young right out of high school. His cousins serve as his best men. The altar behind us is empty. No one willing to hold their peace. Our first kiss tastes of so many lips I cannot distinguish his tongue. He calls me Boo Boo. My heart is warmed. I forget the ways my eyes soot and my skin flames. I rename the feeling devotion. Love, even.

When we are alone, he is small enough to fit in my palms. He reminds me of how he is threat level green when he isn't with them. When I keep things clean. Don't ask questions.

When I mind my own breath. He doesn't red for no reason. I provoke it. I ask where he has been. I ask him where he hasn't. He shifts to fire engine.

The night I finally have enough, he kisses me on my neck. I shudder. He holds my wrists and hisses promises. He tightens. His breath is fermented, and the family resemblance is uncanny. When I do not want to swallow his tongue, he is offended. Pushes my back into the sink. Bends me convex with his weight. Shows me how my hands are laughable prisons. Tangles his hand into my hair and yanks the sense into me.

My hand stretches into the soapy water. Beneath the surface. A pan handle. I almost have it. He bends his other hand into a vise around the scar from the safety pin. His early manifesto. Asks me if I think I am too good for him. When I don't answer, he yells.

My hand ascends. The aluminum chimes against skull. He releases. I swing again. Again. Until he is down. Sangria pouring onto the tiles. I straddle over him, flushed. Just then Death approaches. She is quiet and stands in the archway that leads to the living room. She knows who I am. I want to swing again. She double-grips her scythe. I remember the first time he held me like that. What it felt like to be wanted. I think of what the bed will feel like empty of threat. Still. Cold. Maybe this will teach him his lesson. Maybe he can be reformed. Death close enough to call. Maybe he will awaken a new man.

I tell Death she has come prematurely. I know she is busy. I tell her I will compensate her travel. A plate of salmon croquettes, greens, cornbread. I scoop heavy as she takes a seat at the table. She eats by the handful until she is satisfied. I watch from the seat across from her. She leans over and takes my hand in—gratitude? Pity?

Then the chair isn't beneath me. I am ceiling up and headed for the ground. His hands wrapped around my mouth. The constricting pressure. In my last gasping breath, he tells me I am his. Forever. She sheds a tear and grabs her scythe.

Oh, what fool thinks that they can change Death's mind when she has already made it up? What bigger fool uses hurt to talk themselves out of Love's bet? For every trait that can be criticized as weakness was fashioned for its own purpose. Was not the mind made to forget? Is it not the shield that allows our heart to try again? We may love hard, at times to a fault, but is that not also our gift? That we can fashion a flower from dirt and shit. For what is Love but a seed grown in dying soil. Maybe that too is my grandmother's legacy.

While at the repast, we sit in a sea full of strangers. We take small bites and retell the good parts of my grandfather. The way he brought folks together. His raucous laugh. My grandma, quieter than her usual quiet, sips from his favorite Model T mug and falls deeper into a stare. When we ask her how she is doing, she smiles and nods. The way the drinking bird does. A belly full of rhythmic ink rocking itself against an empty glass behind her. She replays the day he died. Says he told her he was going to renovate their apartment in Heaven. He would see her soon. Told her to take the grandkids traveling. Told her all the things like he always did. Fifty-eight years of telling her what to do. Everything but how to do without him. She went to make him the kind of soup that ails cancer. Heard him collapse in the hallway above before she could get the recipe perfect. She climbs deeper into the glass. Counts all the seconds she could've been in his arms, even when they hurt. Then insists that no man will ever love her like he did. I am sure of that.

When Love finds its end, who is there to move us on? To do the job of dirtying her own hands, even when we are not ready to let go, but Death.

When she comes to claim the soul, Death doesn't always set into her hips. Tired of playing chauffeur. Rushing to end her second shift. Her children, Legacy and Honor, impatiently calling. Her victims begging for more time to do the things Fear talked them out of long ago. She doesn't want mercy. Just wants to have some of the rest she gives. Pouring from an empty stomach can be so fatal. Sometimes, when the dark circles set under her eyes, her restraint slips. She loses peripheral behind the satin hood. Swings her scythe too wide and catches two. A golden cord of no regret. Usually those that love too close for too long. Spouses. Children. Parents. Dragged into afterlife over days, months, a few years. She cannot undo it. Nor do they really want her to. No time or energy to double back. Love waits for her at home ready to grease her scalp. Cook her a hot plate. Reassure her she tried her best. Even when it doesn't seem like enough.

Did I scare you?
Are you usually this afraid of things
you choose not to see?

Going to Church Don't
Make You a Hymnal

Have I lost you? I am sure by now you are wondering why we must dive so deep into Death. Am I addicted to the morbid? Unstable in some way? I would argue that it is the foundation for belief. For what system offers you life without it? What is this land built on if not stolen bones and the stories they couldn't tell? Maybe your discomfort is not with Death, but with what power you lose in accepting it. I would argue that is why we must say her name. For Death does a dirty job no one wants to do. But even Death has regrets. Not of the shepherding to the hereafter, but of the circumstances by which some come to her in the first place. Just as there are justified rounds—age, recklessness, handpicking—Evil heavies her load in ways that are incomprehensible. As my mother would say, "There are some people even Death don't want."

It hadn't been long since Calvary Southern Baptist shed its dusty cream exterior and iconic name for its new identity as Faith of Eagles Christian, my father now at the helm. The building with the fresh baby-blue paint sat on a couple acres of underdeveloped potential in the heart of the Empire. It blended into the highway behind it, back where we used to sneak out of service to play basketball. The quiet bendy street separated the steepleless building from the nearby neighborhood that struggled to bridge to the church despite multiple outreach events. While my father quickly jumped both feet into shepherding, my mother was much more territorial. I would often hear her say, "He's the pastor, God didn't call me to that."

Despite assumptions of what a "First Lady" should be, my mother found no need to keep up the vain appearances. Most Sundays she would dress casually: nice slacks or jeans, a blouse or Christian tee, sandals in the summer or sneakers. It was rarely cooler than sixty degrees in the winter in the desert. On special occasions, anniversaries or special services, she would don suit separates, the occasional dress, but she hated the overfluffed church hats. Even with all Ma'Dea's influence on her, she never joined the Easter Sunday battle for who could block the most children from seeing God. We were nondenominational, so she never had to be one of the one hundred women in white or sit quietly on the front row fawning over my father purely to pacify others' expectations. After all, *she* wasn't the pastor, though her influence was undeniable.

Aside from leading the youth ministry, singing in and part-time directing the praise team, riding with my dad to all his events, meetings, and anywhere someone could accuse him of inappropriate behavior in private, she started a nonprofit through the church. It provided education and resources for families in the community. Offered a safe place for young Black boys with the propensity to end up in jail or dead based on their environments. In some ways, I saw her subsidizing all the hurt between her and my brother by saving someone else's child. She would tuck away into her back office near the fellowship hall and try to absolve herself from church business.

But on Sunday mornings, the lilt in her soprano singing "Blessed Assurance" could tear a new hole in Heaven. My dad's bass would join across the pulpit and blend into the angels' envy. From a young age, I would harmonize in the middle, and together we were the choir. A couple other voices tried supporting us, but I could spot my dad's rumble and my mom's timbre for miles. People often describe marriage as this all-consuming thing. It rarely gives space for a single note to shine. But my parents were more like concurrent solos. My father held together the church while my mother held down the household, the community, homeschooled, and still had time for a Sunday-morning aria. Maybe singing was the way she got through it all. Maybe all the 1950s Roll Tide fashioned in her windpipes made it the easiest place to resist.

Notwithstanding their differences, my parents tried to be a united front. They had a pact—don't embarrass each other—signed in song. So when the newest visiting minister emerged dragging his wife by the wrist and boasting Lucifer's smile, my mother was cordial. He introduced himself before the drove, the way a wolf licks its teeth before feasting. Said to call him Nomed.

My mother always said I had a sense about people; he made my stomach a small boat in a choppy ocean. I didn't know all the facts, but he said he wanted to help. When your congregation is only twenty-five consistent members, you take all the help you can get. And my father was a shepherd. He wanted to gather all the sheep, nurture them, make sure they were full.

My mother, on the other hand, learned early how to become a Kodiak bear: all brawn, claw, and growl when things didn't feel right. Maybe that's how she came to claim my fifth sibling.

My days at the new, more prestigious high school, the one with cement arches and blind corners, the one of first kisses and brute cousins' hands, turned into more daily brawl than learning center. My mother tired of explaining the conflict trinity to the principal and leaving her midday meetings to come and pick me up from school. At the end of the year, she decided to give in to my request and move me away from my brother's campus to the poorer, rival school closer to our home.

PHS wasn't much to look at. The uneven concrete campus sloped to a center, making the quad perfect for flooding in the winter. The unassuming buildings were painted in a deep green that hid the graffiti and mold that we were sure sat in the walls. The library books had pages eaten out by mice, and the textbooks were outdated and still listed Pluto as a planet, back before it wasn't and then it was again. I knew exactly why my mother didn't want me there. But the Friday sock hops and having the worst football team in the region shifted the focus from the jocks to the dancers and artists. I had a chance there. I would no longer be teased for sneaking my spiral of stories from my backpack to add character development or pretty lines. And for all the bullying that the prestigious school offered, PHS offered equal parts friends.

Tabitha introduced herself to me on the first day. She was an awkward Mexicana who you could tell had just left that chola life in the City of Angels by the way her eyebrows were painted on from scratch. Her black hair hung down to her butt, and she always had a scrunchie around her wrist to twist and tail it up in case a fight broke out. She wasn't afraid to take on any challenger, even in orange flip-flops. But balancing out all her quirky confidence was a smile that looked like it had seen the worst and was still determined to push through. I didn't love her at first. She seemed too eager to be my friend, showing up at every passing period and after school to tell me about all the drama I missed freshman year. Before long she started coming home with me for hangouts or lingering in the stands with me for football games where we looked for cute guys on the opposing team.

We rarely went to her home, and the few times we did I learned why. She had been raised by her grandmother, but after her last round, Tabitha moved in with a cousin. There was abuse in that house, though I never saw it. I could smell it in the drywall. I saw it in the way her young cousins flinched when their father moved his hand too quickly toward the table salt. Everyone sat on needles. And while my home offered its own chaos, there was a joy in knowing that we could lay across my waterbed and giggle about the undesirable boys that followed us to Del Taco for a bite after the bell rang. We were best friends, but that didn't stay for long.

A few months after meeting, her cousin decided to move the family closer to the shore. The hours that would span between us would make any postgame moments galivanting evaporate before us. In an effort to maintain some normalcy, she asked if she could move in. My mother and father brought us all together without her for a family meeting.

My mom reminded us, "We don't have much. If we do this, everything that you two kids split will be split between the three of you. You will each have less. But if this is something you want to do, as a family, we will do it."

We all decided that it was better to have her safe with us than beaten down somewhere else. However, she didn't agree. In a weird turn of events, she backed out and moved with her cousin shoreside. And no matter how hard we tried to stay in contact, shifting schedules and stretching hours made keeping our friendship only a great wish.

My family went back to its normal hum: my mother shuttling all of us with the one family car from my brother's school to my father's services to my school for honor roll ceremonies and after-school events. One day, my father was out shepherding someone and my brother decided to walk home from school. As my mother picked me up and moved down her list of errands, she received a call on her cell from my brother. He said he came home to find someone at our home. It was Tabitha. She and all her belongings had been left on our porch with no notice. It seemed her cousin was done trying to raise her and dropped her here for us. From then on, she was never just my friend again. She became my sister. One who laughed me through high school, who my father helped pick out her first car, who shared prom pictures and midnight adventures, who beat out every other mind in our high school to become valedictorian, and who worshipped right beside me every Sunday at Faith of Eagles.

She was there in the weeks leading up to Nomed's emergence. She watched with me as he tried to make the notes between my parents a dissonant chord. He began to prowl like discontent among the other ministers. Soon, they turned on my father, began to say he was incompetent and questioned his caring nature. My father's peace resounded. My mother stood by the stream of them waiting to sink her claws into their skin for swimming against the current. Then they came for her cubs. One minister attacked us in a closed-door meeting saying that we were Hellspawns, allowed to do whatever we wanted, with no respect. My mother started to growl; he didn't know all my parents had done to provide for the three of us. How they had opened their home and settled for less for themselves to make room for another deserving soul. How they bent ends to meet to give me a new school and my brother his own agency. And while my mother had every intention of giving Nomed a piece of her mind, she was calmed by the shepherd's gentle touch. My father switched subjects in hope of delaying the inevitable fight that lingered in every pew. But there is only so long you can let a threat graze before the vibrato sets in.

Soon, it was Sunday morning again. My mother, Tabitha, and I sat in the back row singing and attempting to ignore all the wool and snarl. We had our own hum, passing notes in the back row to our mother's shushing. Snickering at the sleeping deacons in the front row. Before we knew it, the accompaniment tape of the last song ended and the leader of the praise team signaled to begin the welcome. This was a time to acknowledge new guests and embrace old friends.

"If the Jesus in me, meets the Jesus in you, it's so easy . . . so easy to love." There was no one new or easy, and my mother didn't move beyond us. Tabitha and I stood and hugged each other and our mother as the "heys" and "great to see yous" buzzed around us, never quite reaching our pew. Then the growl returned. In the center aisle, with a grin as wide as Judas, came Nomed. He set his eyes on my mother and her cubs.

"Good morning, Sister Pat!"

"Morning."

"I just wanted to let you know that you are the poison that seeps from the sanctuary's walls; a classless condemnation of Christ himself. I bet the devil knows you by your first name. You wretched curse of a woman. Do your children know from what they fell? I pity the thing they call mother."

Right there. In the middle of the welcome. The whole church ignorantly bustled in joy, as if entranced by a spirit so holy it led them to mercy. We are our mother's daughters. Everything in us stood. Tabitha tied her hair up as if a fight was brooding. I prepared to throw the air from my lungs and watch it send him back forty feet. But before we could maul, she grabbed our hands. Our mother stood there, holding us still while the wolf howled and called it hallelujah.

"You, venomous vixen, will welcome God to turn his back on this place. You, your husband, and these things you are raising."

My chest grasped for air, but this time, I couldn't find the melody. I was all rage and teeth. My mother put her paw to my chest as he turned and walked away to greet all the other members who hid in the back rooms to gossip; who paid their tithes and planned their overthrow; who bit the hands and muffled the praises like my mother wasn't one of their only lifelines to God.

Then she found our eyes. She drew back her canines, and she sang. First a slow hum, then a building, audible melody. I don't remember the words, just how light they were. I wanted to belt, to howl, but she held my hand. Tabitha, my mother, and me harmonizing hearts of fury. She stood until everyone was seated but my father at the pulpit. Nomed gloating at his left. I wonder if my father knew the table he was setting before his own enemies. Feeding them all, like he wasn't making the Evil stronger. Like he wasn't leaving my mother out to pasture. A den more deadly than thieves.

Sometimes Evil makes its home in the most holy of places. It waits to turn us into something else. And it is hard to fight it. Maybe because it has always been there. Not in the walls per se, but in the land. We have felt it pulsing beneath our feet. Before belief ever took root, Evil was waiting to hijack the tongue. How else do we explain how we got here? Cargo ships? Loss of Wings? They all answer by the same name. And I must admit I have found comfort in its familiarity once or twice. Played too close to its flames. Thought every translation of its intentions was equal. But this Evil lives off Doubt. And sooner or later, it will make you reckon with it all the same.

If for any moment you count me perfect, know that I don't sell you on that. Every god has made their own mistakes. Own opportunities to pass their wrong choice off as camouflage in the wrong environment. I too have hung around long enough for Evil to sell me a story or two.

Pando's Tin

As the story goes, Pando was very curious.

Maybe it was the order of things for the youngest of seventeen children born stair-step to a mother who started at twenty. Wasn't no room for coddling at the bottom of the totem pole. Had to figure out a way for yourself. And Pando was the kind of child who didn't bruise easily. He cut his teeth on bits of ham hock and mustard greens at six months when his mother's breast finally ran dry. Learned how to soothe his own cry by rocking himself to sleep. He was all things exceptional, ahead of his class, would dismantle things around the house just to see their inner workings. Clocks. Telephones. Lamps. Hearts. All lay in Pando's warpath as he attempted to dissect how everything worked. Never quite knew how to put them back together, but guess that's why he had Grandma Mae. And oh, was he the apple of his grandmother's pie.

She would often keep him when his mother and father needed a break from the chorus of stair-step voices all sounding like a collateral choir through every pore of the house that tilted down on Rider St. Each child parceled out to various godparents, friends, and family to thin the herd. And Pando always landed in Grandma Mae's welcoming arms.

She lived close by. Down by where the neighborhood women ran the Saturday morning farmer's market. Pando would often accompany her to get the newly spun yarn and fresh vanilla for the tea cakes she baked to celebrate his arrival. Grandma Mae noticed early the way that the neighbor women looked down at Pando—a coy smirk creeping through their cheeks, as his soft almond hands tinkered with something he'd pocketed for later dismantling. He always got her an even better deal when it came to the pricing. Every heart is a sucker for a cute kid with a smile. And Pando's just about broke open the earth. Some kind of powerful doe-eyed gleam of white that almost blinded you. Put you in a trance. But Pando didn't quite know how to use it yet. Flashing it at every older woman who tried to pinch his cherub cheeks or who offered him something sweet just for a chance to see it. Grandma Mae tried her best to guard all that light, but some things just can't be hidden under a bushel.

Once they got what they needed, Pando and Grandma Mae would make their way back to her place to bake. She would line the counter with parchment and flour while he washed his hands from all that tinkering. Then, though they had engaged in the ritual dozens of times, she would show him how to measure and knead and roll as if he had never done it before—and he would let her. Maybe for attention. Maybe to make sure he had done it right. Maybe for no other reason but the curiosity to see if she would change something, which she did every time, just a smidge. A little more butter, a little longer whip. Pando noticed everything.

Those tea cakes were the kind of thing that made the whole house smell like hunger and buffered Pando's endless questions. While the oven grew the small morsels of dough into sweet confections, Grandma Mae would sit near the window, crocheting some unidentifiable garment, while Pando bounced between asking questions and sneaking up on the oven to try to peek in.

"Boy, you're letting all the heat out!" Grandma Mae would rebuke between stitches.

Sending Pando flying across the room to hide his curiosity.

But it ever itched.

"Gramma, why is the sky blue? And why don't dogs have arms? And what would happen if the sun burned up? Would it get real dark?"

"We would die, Pando. Go on to be with the Lord on that great wrap around in the sky."

She would explain what she could while he bounced between subjects with anticipation until the egg timer rang and the cookies were done and she clinched the needles mid-stitch cause her Pando had a hankering for something sweet.

After donning the farm-plaid oven mittens and pulling the pan from the oven, Grandma Mae would send Pando to the pantry to get a tin to store it in. The back wall of the deep closet was filled with all kinds of things. Glass jars of preserved jellies. Unlabeled cans of mysterious rations. And on the top shelf, sat the Forbidden Tin. Blue and round with images of spiraled shortbread and paper-wrapped sugar squares. Seemed like the perfect thing to use to store tea cakes, but Grandma Mae said not to touch it. Pando never understood why. It just sat there, towering over him as his hands began to itch with intrigue.

"But why can't I use the blue one, Gramma?"

"Because I said so. Now come on back in here before I eat all of these cookies by myself."

And every time he considered it again, right at the point where he would decide this was the day he was gonna scale the shelves and get it, Grandma Mae would see him with her second eyes and call his attention back to the red-lidded Tupperware on the pantry floor. And just like that, he would lose the nerve, knowing she would come look for him soon, knowing she was the only one ever looking for him. So he would grab the largest plastic shape from beneath the grocery bags and head back to the kitchen.

But he never forgot the tin.

Every week, he would stare up at it. And every week it seemed to get closer. Maybe it was his imagination. Maybe it was the way that boys seem to stretch taller every time you see them. Maybe it was the delay in how long it took Grandma Mae to call his name. She seemed slower on the uptake now—most days, making Pando do all the baking while she supervised from a stool near the sink. The clink of crochet needles becoming sluggish in pace but unrelenting. The length of weave billowing now down the hallway. He never quite knew what she was making, but it never seemed done, even as his questions deepened.

"Gramma Mae, how did you know when it was right to tell Grandpa you loved him? Do you still miss him? Do you think I will die young too?"

Grandma Mae breathed deeply and kept on crocheting.

"I can tell you that Love and Death are both unpredictable. All you can do is love as hard as you can until you can't. Just the way I do you, Pando."

Once reassured, he would help her to the seat near the bay window where they would nibble, share secrets, and seam together all of his unraveling curiosities as they watched the folks pulse down the busy street. The street that seemed to shift from farmer's market to strip mall to farmer's market in a strip-mall parking lot. Pando was older now, but not old enough to know how precious each second spent in that window was becoming. Until one day, Grandma Mae was replaced by a sea of bodies in black, buzzing around her kitchen, scavenging from aluminum trays of memories and leftovers, like they had known Mae the way that he did.

That day, when they gave her body to the earth, in the heat of the grieving, Pando remembered her hands. He remembered the way she sifted the flour between her knuckles, the way she laughed at every joke, the way she let him lick the spoon they used to stir it all together, the way she always had an answer for every question that plagued him. He smiled, before wondering, "Who would answer them now?"

He just needed to hold onto her a little longer, watch her pull one more strand through what seemed like an unfinished tapestry that now lay discarded in a box under the windowsill, just out of sight. It was this need for something that still tasted of those memories that led him to the pantry.

He didn't even remember heading there, he just wanted to get away from the hordes of familial strangers apologizing for his loss like the whole world shouldn't be grieving. He panned the dimly lit room, hoping to find a leftover morsel, something to fill the belly-aching void he now felt. Something to keep him warm with her love. It was then that he saw the tin. It now sat at eye level. He knew he shouldn't open it, but there was no one left to tell him no. He was a young man now, one raised under Grandma Mae's tutelage. One who had questions and an itch that had been growing for years. An itch that now thrust his hands up and onto the metal tin. He could hear her for a moment.

"Ah ah ah . . . don't you use that one, Pando."

"But why, Gramma? But why?"

No hooks clinked. No garment grew. No answer returned. He sat down on the pantry floor. Hesitating slightly as his fingers curled around the outer lip of the lid, and for a moment, he thought he heard Grandma Mae calling, but then the silence. He sat waiting for someone to come, but wasn't nothing but that itch in the middle of his palms. So Pando took one giant breath, and pulled it open.

Upon first glance, the tin seemed all but empty. Just a gleam of two small pieces of silver at the bottom. Pando leaned in, looking for some trace of something else. Had she merely meant to test his self-control all those years? Then he noticed that these weren't ordinary pieces of metal. No, these were miniature crochet hooks, no bigger than the tip of his finger. They looked just like the ones that would slide between her hands as the wisdom slipped from her lips. But they seemed to be stuck down, glued against the bottom of the tin. He slid his nail against the metal and pried them free. No sooner than he did, did they begin to vibrate.

The hooks shook with such ferocity that they seemed to levitate with their own spirit. Pando watched, doe eyes growing wider, smile starting to burst from his face upon seeing magic firsthand. Then, the first hook latched into his chest with a searing quickness. It happened so fast that Pando didn't have time to pull it free before the other hook darted across the room, into the leftover yarn, and began yanking. Pando's widening eyes flashed with terror as the first hook pulled his skin back, leaving his rib cage exposed. Adrenaline. That must've been the reason he couldn't feel the hook digging into his open chest, weaving the opening stitch under and over ribs. He finally snapped out of the daze and began trying to pry the hook free. But out of thin air, the yarn turned red hot and started fastening things down.

Happiness was the first to go. Maybe because it was already weakened under the loss of Grandma Mae. The yarn tangled around every budding smile as the color washed out of Pando's face. Then the aching pain of Joy seeping out. Like someone was draining all of the strength from his legs. Next, he began to seize as the Hope was enveloped. He fell over thrashing for an ounce of strength. Empathy was next. A numbing creeping all over his body. Then Curiosity slipped. He stopped caring why this was all happening, he just wanted the pain to stop. The Sadness was last. It sobered him briefly. For a moment he almost convinced himself that this was all a dream. That Grandma Mae lay on the other side of that door. That he could still smell the cookies. But he couldn't move and that enraged him.

In a second wind, he found himself emboldened. His body seemed engulfed in anger. It may have been the only thing that saved him. He crawled to his knees yanking the hooks free from his chest. His sweaty hands flung them across the room and covered the now gaping hole with the lid to the tin. The hooks seemed to linger in rhythm, looking for a way in a chest that now puffed and swelled around the tin lid making it immovable. Then began the drumming. The eternal tremble of the hooks as if they were knocking to gain entry. Each tinny thump fueling the rage even more until all Pando saw was red.

From then on, no matter how hard he tried to laugh or cry or feel, all of it just came out hot. Like he was still trying to quiet the noise or fight it all off. Like there would never be anyone worthy enough to reach in and loosen the threads.

Pando finally understood what his Grandma Mae was trying to protect him from. See, it's not things getting out that we should fear, but it's all of the things we hold in.

The first time I held a gun was at a chapel. Not in the building, but on the loose gravel we deemed a neutral parking lot between the cholos and the saved folk. I don't know how I got out of service, but I know it wasn't one of the evenings my parents forced me to wait while parishioners raided the food pantry or dropped off clothes for our annual clothing giveaway. This was smack in the middle of "Say that, Pastor" and "Amen," holy howling and "the blessing to the reading and hearing of the Word." My brother and I gathered out front around our friend Chris's car.

Chris belonged to the street, a wayward teen my father was trying to win over to Christ. His greased black hair gelled against his head or all over the place, rarely anywhere in between. He brandished neck and hand tattoos and drove his own car. He was kind, and sweet, and reckless. Had a smile that could make his mother forgive him. I think he lived with her, but I also remember an argument about him getting thrown out. He was lowrider smooth in a black

Chevy Cavalier. My brother was still acclimating to teen-agehood, but too old to be treated like a child. Just trying to keep the street credit he thought he lost when my parents left the City of Angels and moved to the desert of Inland Empire. He clung to Chris's rebellious familiarity. I wasn't always allowed with them, but this Sunday they didn't shoo me away as usual.

My father and Chris had a deal: the gun doesn't come into the church. Despite most reputations of most street folk, they are usually fairly respectful and are very loyal to their word. So when Chris agreed, he stuck to it. But that didn't mean he didn't look for loopholes. And Evil always finds a loophole. The parking lot was not *in* the church.

I remember walking up to the passenger side of his black four-door sedan. He squatted down and pulled a black bag from underneath the seat. He closed the door and carried it back to the trunk where he opened it and laid out the contents. He assembled the unfamiliar pieces as my brother's eyes lit up with adoration. By now we had been gone long enough for someone to wonder where we were. I kept watching the door and listening for the rise and fall of my father's bass. Every time the small congregation got too quiet, or there were too many shadows moving behind the yellow-frosted stained glass, I got nervous. But Chris and my brother were too in tune with the grip and barrel to ever consider getting caught.

Chris leaned over to my brother and said, "Wanna see the best part?"

Chris flipped a switch and a red light danced on his out-
stretched hand. Both boys smiled.

My brother had to be next. He held the gun in both his
hands and stared at it like it was some sort of moral decision. Then he cocked it sideways, like he had seen in *Menace
II Society*. He aimed it at the back half of the L-shaped building, down where the treasurer would meet after church to
count the money. *Pew, pew* . . . He mocked the sounds of it
firing and pretended to be retaliating on a rival threat.

I stuck my hand out where they couldn't ignore it. "Can I
try?" I asserted myself as not to give them reason to think I
was a punk or scared or any less experienced with firearms
than I was with dolls. Chris took the gun from my brother's
hands and gently placed it in mine. My hands instantly
braced. I remember how heavy it was in my palms. How I
had to hold with two hands around the grip, two fingers on
the trigger. I let the red dot dance farther in, near the nurs-
ery, the classroom where the kids learned about Heaven. Up
the main hall, near the pulpit, the wolf's seat next to it. I
wondered how anyone could be strong enough to carry this
in the small of their back without being weighed down so
much that they couldn't move. I wondered what it would feel
like to shoot, the controlled click and splatter, harpooning
a wild dog with a precise caliber, but would I dare let it fire?

Before I could fully form a verdict, Chris took it from
my hands and told me to be careful. Guns only make permanent decisions. He carefully wrapped it back in its body

bag and stowed it under the seat. He promised that next time we could take it out back, near the freeway where no one could hear, and shoot cans off the fence. My brother mumbled something about ditching the girl, but Evil's hunger had already taken hold of me.

The sound of the closing hymn marked the end of prayer. Soon they would be looking for us, so I headed back inside. The sanctuary was a buzz of lightheartedness: people hugging and encouraging each other to hold on to God throughout the week. Bodies undulating like red-dotted monkeys for a carnival prize. I faded between the pews, just wanting to be lost and not where everyone smiled a falsehood and wished you well only while you were looking. My mouth left holding a magazine full of anger with nowhere to empty. After all, we were in the Lord's house, and enough of me still knew better.

My mother always said, "If you let Evil ride shotgun, eventually he will want to drive." And if he drives, he won't take you somewhere that is easy to come back from. So part of me learned how to talk the Evil out. But this land always makes room for it to sprout somewhere. In the dark corners of suburbia or the dank underbellies of the interwebs, Evil squats, keeping a long list of people and places that wouldn't let him stay. Ones he forces Death to take. And, oh, how the houses of the Lord become a fitting place to return with all violence in Evil's hand. O Birmingham, O Mother Emanuel, must we sing of this same story again?

A Hymn for the Ambushed

♪ *I couldn't hear nobody prayin'*
Lord, I couldn't hear nobody prayin'
When I went down yonder
By myself and
I couldn't hear nobody prayin'
Lord ♫

[1]Upon entering your church, the devil don't appear out of place. [2]Remember, he was once an angel, still remembers how to sing. [3]How to hold a harmony in his cheek: a dirty tobacco. [4]How to ride a hymn of rage through hours of traffic, only to cloak himself sheep familiar, enter into our fellowship halls. [5]We welcome him like the saints we don't know we are becoming. [6]Sit him close as kin, want him to feel this Jesus all over him. [7]Shiver in the room—Holy Ghost? [8]*Didn't know this fear made flesh to walk among us.* [9]We sit a semiautomatic away, judgment held on tongue, hollow point. [10]We sway in unison. [11]*Didn't know fury was coming.* [12]*Didn't know repentance had a skin color.* [13]Sanctuaries aren't made for shootings. Bibles aren't made to catch bullets. [14]He holds my hand in prayer as if we have the same father. [15]Looks square in my flesh and can't bear the Black forgiveness. [16]*Who knew Wednesday nights were made for weeping?* [17]No

joy cometh in our mourning. [18]The shots. [19]All organ strings break at once. [20]The shots. [21]A fleeting exodus of guardians wings. [22]We scream. [23]No amen in tremble; no duck and pray. Chaos. Our bodies slain. Wrong spirit. Savior? Show up? Survival? [24]If I paint myself in the blood, will he confuse me for Passover? [25]Make yourself invisible. [26]Most people shoot straight. [27]Hold my firstborn's cooling hand, life leaving fast. [28]Mother's voice? Hallelujah?

God our Father? Don't let him see us. [29]With each inching step, I try not to cringe. [30]Control my blinks. Breaths. Psalms pouring from my palms. [31]He pauses: a thief in the night looking for one more colored soul to leave cold-boarded on this chapel floor. [32]Wait! [33]Must be an uneasy conviction pushing him out. God's eye watching as he runs from grace. [34]The floorboards quiet hundred-year-old mouths. Hum of AC. Soul fading into a muffled corpse of silence.

♪ I couldn't hear   Nobody   prayin'

Lord,   I couldn't hear ♫

Nobody

Nobody

Evil makes a victim of Death in her own home. Leaves a trigger under the front porch. Waits for the boom, one Death can't help but feel, and lets her count each body raining down. Watches her name each massacre after the faith that used to be there. Each face grafted onto her cloak. After enough gathering, she must empty some. Even Death has her limits. She has found a place for the ones that are only remembered by name, decades later.

There, behind the house that held my mother's childhood sprawl, in the resting place for once-ebony corpses. The field of blooming concrete angels. She buries those destined to return. Left to suck sap until the next reunion, seventeen years in the making. There are many vineyards like this, littered in the area. Places Death dusts off, emerges from walking the earth's crust. Meeting Evil's quick hands and light feet with discernment and grace.

She met my grandmother in her seventies. Collected the memories Evil knocked from her in the first round. Once delirious, Death called the fight. Put her out of her dragging misery. Pulled the golden cord of my grandfather's name until she was yanked home with him.

My grandfather made it three rounds with Evil. They say the ones who last longer must retain a certain meanness. Like my mother's great-grandmother. Mastered button pushing, backhanded compliments. Anything that cut out the sweet. Delayed Death's final judgment.

My Gma has gone no less than six rounds with Evil.

Once in the City of Druids, a few times in the City of Motors, even tried in the City of Angels. But my Gma just gritted her teeth. Doubled down on the harsh tone. Cut out all the fluff. Shoots straight. Keeps on pushing back.

I worry when we don't speak. I know how relentless Evil can be, how Death won't take the sufferer's route. That somewhere in there, my Gma's love for the Lord and her kind heart will be her undoing. Even Evil knows his greatest weapon is Fear. And everyone knows where kindness is based. Irrevocably. It is the reason we love. Who is Love but the avoidance of dying alone? What is loneliness but the fear of your own mind? Of the softness of your own body? So when Gma offends, when she snaps at an unmade bed or a loud child, we know she is reassuring us and Death that she is not ready to lose. That there is less fear in her voice today than yesterday. To convince Death, you must have no fear left. Which also means no kindness. Not even a mustard seed. This is why the old care little. Why the mean live long. Why the young die young. Were it not for the fear, we may all be immortal.

But youth may be the greatest deceiver of them all. Evil has learned to strike while the blood pumps fast. It is why we fear for ourselves but fear more for our children.

When my daughter goes missing in
the way children often do,
When she narrows her body

between clothing racks
in a department store or arcs the covers over
her head for too long,
I have no choice but to consider Death
may be watching.

When she dances too gracefully,
Runs too fast for the shudder
of the street, I wonder if Evil
is a blot away.
Oh, the lessons I have tried to teach
that a loud mouth won't eat long.

That a sound sleep is too
familiar a posture,
a raided home abstract.
That a video game played
too long is a prime moment your
own head may be lost to sketch.

Our kind have met Death
on a less-perfect canvas, but it is not
a care of hers
How a mother's mourning may draw a crowd
if Death does what she must—
the gracious final draft.

Youth pays the future no mind.
If it will come it will.
But what to do with the pain of
knowing that every move

is a tortured inspiration?
Even when she didn't know
She was being drawn.

This, a mother's burden. Knowing that even the ones birthed from us struggle to believe us. But what is faith if it always ends in Death? What is life if it doesn't go on? I refuse to only offer you Fear and undoing. This land promises enough of that. But what of the space after life. That which is prime for rebirth. How else can I reassure you we have lived and died to live again? Even in the wake of our own loss, we have found a way to hope. Maybe I only recognize now that it has been there all along. I want to go back and gather the memories learned by the graveside. I want to recount their names in a new light. Conjure new ways to reclaim or reincarnate.

My sister Denise ascended when I was eight. I remember because the summer was more humid, the porches heavier in song. Monique took flight five summers ago; we blamed cancer in the summer of a hurricane. She waited in the tree in my backyard while my city flooded just to croak goodbye.

My father has lost two daughters to the seasons. My family knows well what the summer brings, even my Gma.

In the years I straddled childhood and adulthood equally, she sat at the grave site, long after her son's, my uncle's, casket was visible, just waiting to see how the ground would receive him. Long after the procession of aunts using sunglasses to hide their tears had come and gone. Long after one of them threw herself on top of the mahogany box suspended over the hungry plot. The nice lady with the white gloves had to forcibly remove her after she begged God to take her too. She never means it. My grandmother built her body into his headstone. Open-armed parent of missing prodigal. Waited for the friend who shot him to rewind time and reconsider. Waited for his son to unsee his collapsing father before him. Waited.

He descended into the earth on his son's first birthday. My grandmother helped plan a party to replace the wake. It was full of unfamiliar family and flowers and pictures of a man who won't be home before some unknown summer. They talked about when he was young and all the hearts he broke. My grandmother's. They left out the guns, the blackened lips and bright bandanas, the way she prayed her knees callused, the way the streets devoured, the way he had to run 1,300 miles to start over, the way it caught up to him. My Gma dreaded all the talking. She dug her hand into the earth. The way a queen buries a pharaoh. Wanted to feel for any movement. She reminded him that her heart was a tree that he would always be welcome to sing from. And when there were no more prayers left to pray, my grandmother gathered her body that created life once. Even if it is not still able. She promised to visit him, there, in the large oak at the top of the hill. She smiled and did not say goodbye.

Even if all we have is a story, we still have that. And, oh, what a blessing that is. So when my daughter asks me, "What happens after you die?" I do not have to be conflicted. Though the cross on my heart wants to tell her of pearly gates and the streets full of gold, this thing that helped us survive the field, this hope, I don't have to give in to white-washed mansions on large plots of land, where worship looks like work. I hear the drumbeat in me, the one that wants to give her a Heaven that doesn't sound like a plantation. But I cannot change that we are what and where we have always known. Maybe I can still give her a story that sounds like us.

To God's Ears

There was once a woman who loved her daughter more than her heart would allow. The two were inseparably Black. They would go everywhere together. The beauty shop, the grocery store, church seven days a week; they breathed each other's smiles. Their favorite place was the community garden behind their house. The land opened up just past the mature oaks. Long ago, their grandmother planted all kinds of magic that bloomed every year for all the neighbors to enjoy. The mother and daughter would sit among the coiled vines and eat cherry tomatoes by the handful. They would scoop up the earth and bury seeds of new life. Then they would water it again and again until the green sprouts broke ground and promised something fresh. They would lose hours on back porches watching as the sun set over the high stalks and heavy sunflowers. Once it was too dark to see their feet against the sod, they would retreat to the shotgun house where the lanterns burned kerosene rich until the sandman came to drop off dreams. The mother would stretch long across the couch with her head near the screen door to hear any racoons or high winds trying to get in.

On Saturday mornings, the daughter would rise to the smell of thick bacon bought at Johnson's Market up the dirt road where the goldenrods swathed the fields into a gilded sea. Her mother warmed the sweet-glassed molasses in a pot of water on the stove. A short stack of corn cakes ready to topple on the table. Just the kind of food that fuels an entire day. When their bellies were full and their sugar was high, they would slip on their gloves and rush back to the garden. The screen door would croak upon its hinges, both bodies lunging back into the heat, bursting from the tree line to water the soil with their sweat until it bred life. A regular harvest of smiles at the slightest hint of melon or pepper, then the darkness and the creak of that screen door welcoming them back. Mother on the couch. Daughter tucked tight in her bed.

The early morning would ring like a church bell. The

mother would rise to lay out doily socks and frilly pink dresses, clip buxom bows into the daughter's hair, and fasten her own hat big enough to shade this side of earth. This was the Lord's Day and they would head to meet him at the chapel at the end of the street. After they had sung themselves tired, they would find their second wind at the creak of that old back door. Their white gloves pulling it wide to get all the frills in without tearing. In the breath of an ox, both traded all the pomp for torn jeans and gardening gloves and took to the wind in full sprint toward their personal Eden. God lived there too, they were sure.

One evening, after the sun seemed to hold a grudge against the outside, they found themselves more drained than usual. They both barely made it into the house without toppling over onto each other. Their skin, more bronzed, seemed to hold all the light it was given for itself. The daughter, dirty and smiling, never made it to her bed. She collapsed on the couch just past the threshold. The mother couldn't bring herself to wake her. She nestled in the daughter's bed, slipping deeper into dream. Her ears snuggled tight into the soft pillow. So tight she didn't hear the wind come in. Or the Evil that followed. The uniform of privilege. The muffled scream. The flailing feet. The daughter's failed clawing of her own life out of their hands. The screen croaked for help, as the silence and their hands swallowed her deep down the road.

The next morning, the mother rose. She laid out the ruffled socks neat and clean on the bed, fluffed the rose tulle on the daughter's favorite Sunday dress, and headed for the kitchen. The house was an eerie reverb. An empty table and hollow floors. Breakfast beckoned in its usual way. About halfway through the sizzle, she realized the couch was empty. She called out for her daughter, assuming she had risen early, but found the soot-dusted blanket yanked across the floor. Then the croak and bang, the back door opening and closing by itself. The mother thought maybe her daughter had headed to the garden without her. She ran through the garden, seeing no trace of her. She went door to door asking the neighbors if they knew what happened. No one willing to say what she already knew. Until she arrived at the last house on the block. This time, an older woman answered the violent knocking. But before the mother could finish asking, the older woman grabbed her in an embrace and she felt virtue leave her body. She staggered back home with all knowing. Her empty arms longing to hug her child, to feel the buzz of her breath against her chest. For the unjust lost always leave behind longing. An answer grown in the gut. By the time she arrived at the house, her legs could no longer hold the denial. She crumpled against the porch, wailing.

For the next year, her body curled around itself, trying to remember what it felt like to be full. By the time fall closed its eyes, shock had moved to grief. The kind that says that the whole world was gonna move on, even if she couldn't. She refused to eat. Wrapped in the blanket that still held the dust of her daughter's last laugh all winter, she succumbed to the couch all spring. Then summer brought a familiar croak. Startled, she looked to the back door, thinking the Evil had returned to steal more coal for its next altar. By now the evenings had shortened and the late-day darkness had settled in thick. It was hard to see outside, but something was summoning her. She unfurled her body long enough to grab a small cast-iron skillet from the kitchen to defend herself. Then she went to investigate. She pushed the door open wide and called out, "Who's there?"

Shuffling footsteps broke through the sounds of the night. Death put two feet square on the porch. The mother grabbed her cloak and fell to her knees. She begged Death to take her too, but Death did not oblige. Death pulled the mother up and pointed out toward the garden in the distance. The moon lighted the path down past the tree line. They walked together out to the resting soil where no plants were grown. Death knelt down. She reached into her cloak and pressed something to the earth. Then touched the mother's chest. A croak seemed to resound from the soil. The mother knelt too now, placing her hand against the ground, only to feel a flitter. Then the earth began a subtle tremble. Her eyes widened with expectation as the ground broke open to announce life. A nymph emerged. It shook off the dust. Then began scurrying away. The mother followed it as it jostled its heavy casing through the greens, past the ripening orbs of sweet, to the base of the nearby trees, before rapturing up to take its place among the branches. She watched it undress only to emerge a cicada: divine wings and a new body.

Within moments, its chest bulged into song. It was a familiar croak. The same one she heard when the back door swung wildly at her daughter's bursting. The same song her daughter's hungry belly sang on Sunday mornings before worship. The same one that would swell on every front porch when the summer was high and the loss rate was higher. Here, in the trees, was resurrection. The glorious moonlight luminescing through paper wings. Her daughter's new seraphic face with eyes wide enough to watch the entire garden multiplying into harvest. Her mother's chest filled as the cicada took flight, only to land just above her heart.

This sweet surrender at Death's hands. The mother exhaled goodbye before watching her daughter ascend. The stars ignited and the entire sky filled with song. Each tree's dwelling joining in chorus, vibrating drums in tymbal, a tribal welcome.

Branch to branch, child to child. From our mouths to God's ears.

And ain't this our own kind of Heaven.

Woman, sing yourself out of the funk.
You are a new suit on a clean body
Wear yourself out!

We Got It Honest

At least it is our hope. That this world would have at least one safe place for our bodies. For Joy lives in the body. A menagerie of divine vessels stain-glassing under our own blacklight. Still finding a way to be vibrant without apology. To be fragile and unbreakable. What a tricky thing it is, becoming fluorescent when all eyes are looking for a flaw.

There are certain pigments
no one expects.

They say Black means recluse,
willing to eat her own shade, a
sign of depression,
Death's first cousin—
never removed.

That sometimes when we
have too much
light, we swallow our own
shadows, shape-shift the sun in smile,
become a spectrum of shades
burning off.

The lonely silence
of being the coal all
want to burn for fuel.

Maybe the Black was
always under there,
all the other colors
just camouflage.

We become what we must to survive. Maybe this is why we are reborn every morning. Maybe we never really die; never been damaged either. Just formed. All this pressure shaping us into something worth listening to. Like a story enduring the edits. What Joy hasn't suffered long? What body hasn't borne the brunt? For a martyr is not revered for the way that they died, but for all the Joy that encamped on either side of the suffering. I have no greater proof than the way my mother smiles.

Through aching back. Broken under a stepchild's yoke. Carpeted against the zebra-striped poof. Sunken under the piling dishes. Belt in one hand, Bible in the other. Alone, wishing her God a dream catcher. Enveloped by her children's sin. Repenting for her own Doubt. Her body sprawled before the TV or pressed to the sliding glass door. Sun warming her skin to toasted bronze with not a penny to compare. Joy needs nothing to possess, crawls inside her like a chill. Pulls the strings of her curtain mouth until the light bursts through. Her gap that spans the heavens, makes passage for the kind of laugh that gushes out. Unapologetic. Cheekbone mountains in bounding fog of guffaw. Tears streaming down at an off-color joke. Or as a lap full of child squirms in tickle. And her mouth is the Red Sea letting it all out.

This may not be the arrival you have been waiting for. But the only notion I can cosign is that Joy doesn't ask permission from Sorrow. They are symbiotic lovers entangled in each other. One body feeding off itself in perfect balance. Looking over itself like a worthy sacrifice. One I have lived more times than any mortal can count.

Once the house and the six-figure income were gone, my parents struggled to find a safe place to call home. After considering many options, including a demon-possessed shack near my grandparents' rural getaway, they committed to a split-level up near City of Wildfires, just outside the Empire. The dusty hill land was endless, offering homes an acre apart and the kind of lots that were the perfect scene for a horror movie. But don't be confused, this was not land of wealth. It was a land that had been burned down so many times before that people stopped investing in rebuilding it. My parents found a house to rent, barely standing between the tumbleweeds. Carcass of shelter draping itself over us. When I speak of it now, I choke a little on the ash.

I was ten then, and I can still feel the shag carpet under my feet. A mustard yellow that stretched across the living room and right up to the linoleum floor. It had four bedrooms, separated by wings. My brother and I at one end of the house, with a bathroom to share, and my parents at the other end. A living room and a kitchen between us. Our fridge rarely held more than potatoes and Dijon mustard that my father insisted on having even though he was never really there to eat it. But it didn't matter, because my room was the coolest architectural nonsense in the world. I had three square walls and one that was round and bent, where you could roll across it like it was a valley. It was a joy to paint when my father gave in and let me drench it in sky blue. I wanted to feel like I could fly. Maybe I could. I don't remember the inside of my brother's room. Probably because I wasn't allowed in. Now a teenager, he didn't want me to find the weed he was hiding from my parents. Maybe he was searching for flight too.

My mother tended to linger on her side of the house. She occasionally emerged to make dinner or share a laugh. I do not know what her room looked like. We weren't allowed in. I figured it was because there was no one else to see. My father, by then more pastor than present. I assumed she used her room to hide from the rising hormones of my brother and the missing hand of my father.

My favorite place was the backyard. There was a giant oak tree that shaded over everything. It was so big that the previous tenants had hung a rope from one of the thickest branches. My brother and I would take turns wrapping the twine around our stomachs and launching each other across the sprawl of the shaded canopy. We would crash just short of the giant mulberry tree. We would sit there for hours, blue-blacking our hands with the sticky-sweet juice.

My mother pushed us to play outside as much as possible. Maybe she just wanted to see if we would ever master a superpower. Maybe because my brother and I were creative and amicable there. We would play G.I. Joe versus Barbie in the land of the giants. Inevitably Barbie would be captured in G.I. Joe's war camp. Then all the other toys that my brother collected for the stop-animation films he was now obsessed with creating would jump in to help save her. There would be Street Sharks skating into the opening of the Cave of Wonders, where Tigger and Midge would plot to get Barbie back. We once built an internment camp for Winnie-the-Pooh. Real Acirema shit. We buried Pooh underground for an entire winter. When we dug him up, he was covered in black roaches and dust. Still smiling. We built adventures out of daylight. My mother would be a ghost at the sliding glass door.

At night we would retreat to our rooms to read or would sometimes play a game together. Our favorite was taking bets on if the lights would stay on. We would ante up toys as collateral and watch the clock. If it made it to five p.m. and the lights were still on, the light company would let us keep power for the weekend. If not, we would break out the candles and Pictionary. By the time we set it up, my father would be home. He would often indulge us with a poorly drawn giraffe before kissing my tired mother sweetly and heading to bed. She would exhale the day at a touch of his lips. Shortly after, she would retreat to meet him at their end of the house, and we to ours.

My mother didn't speak of the black mold she spent hours cleaning in quiet or the bleach that lightened her hands no matter how many gloves she wore. She did not explain how much danger she kept at bay for us. She made a choice, to put her hope in us, again and again. That one day our arms would be strong enough to lift us all out. That we would remember all the bruised ribs and busted knees as the runway that showed us how hard learning to fly could be.

Where one may hear this as poverty, we see all the joy that lives here too. What is the world but a contradiction we are trying to navigate? Moments eaten with delight and wincing, one after another. Oh, this body full of recluse and wander, forgive me for not rejoicing. For wishing you were anything else. For the young envy the wisdom of the old, but not the body. The old, seasoned of mind, miss their spryness.

And I have not been the only one preoccupied with holding on to youth, as if it is the only way to truly know Joy.

To Keep from Crying

Some envy dimples. Others large, offset eyes. But everyone wants to be young. To preserve the taut skin and glow, some seek a safe life. But this is where they all go wrong. They do not understand what it takes to turn your face into polished marble.

Medusa knew. They turned her dreadlocked poise into a serpentine monster.

But all of us know of Zora, Goddess of Youth. She finds you at the first sign of trauma, when you are too naive to believe in the ugly of people and too hurt to move. The ache throbs fresh within you. Then your age is not a number but a point of return. Your tears are as pure and honest as your laugh. She catches each one in the palms of her hands. The way a leaf cradles the dew in the morning light. Shapes all of your fragile into an ankh. A cross. Whatever faith keeps you safe. Presses it deep into your sternum, where the child blood pulses stronger. Where an offering of a laugh, one true and gut-wrenching, can reignite it to make your face a lush field of copper or bronze or cast-iron stunning. Where, each time that danger comes for you and you laugh to keep from crying, you are reborn.

This is what they have spent years in search of. This way to siphon all the pain into something usable. To ward off the wrinkles that tell of each time they have been knocked down and shattered just a bit. They don't understand how the Joy only knows itself once it is plunged into the river of agony. But you have always been an aqueduct, my dear. One straight to the feet of God. And trauma can be such a fountain of youth.

That's why Black don't crack. But it sure does bend awful close. I tell you this not out of pride, but out of failure first. If only you knew how many times I have blossomed into a new body only to curse it too. I have lived, no fewer than ten lifetimes, as an imposter in my own skin. One who punished herself for not fitting into a land that was never built for me. I can show you better than I can tell you.

Before students transitioned into their adult lives, our school offered them one last hoorah on the school's senior trip to Six Flags. I finagled a few free tickets "as chaperone" in exchange for barely watching a hundred eighteen-year-olds tackle some of the best roller coasters three hours outside Space City in the State of Lonely Stars. While I had been on most of their coastal versions, I was excited to ride the Wonder Woman ride that had come out the previous year. Wonder Woman has always been my favorite. She was one of the first strong images of a badass woman I saw growing up. *And* she had an invisible plane. I remember seeing the early cartoons where she had pronounced hips and bulging muscles. She showed that a woman didn't have to be this frail, petite damsel in distress, but she could be a god in her own right—have the power to define how the world bowed to her.

On the way up, I talked to all my previous students about the rides they wanted to tackle and how much we had all needed a break from any educational stimuli. The school had set up a group chat for the students to communicate with teachers throughout the day and get important information. However, by hour two, it turned into pictures of kids caught sleeping, the ever-timely meme about the charter-bus bathroom, and pictures of teachers caught candid in class that they had been saving all year. Most of it was hilariously inappropriate, but it made for a good ride. When we arrived, the students rushed the picnic area for lunch.

As we were gathering our belongings and students, Lupe, who was also chaperoning, admitted that he'd never ridden a roller coaster before. My mission was clear: get all of us on something fast. But since he insisted on low thrills, I headed for the moderate coaster in the back of the park.

The kids quickly ditched us, leaving a small pack of adults to relive our glory days of revelry. We darted to the back of the park, surveying all of the rides we planned to conquer on the way. Lupe pointed out all the loop-de-loops and death-defying heights he would never try. I looked on with excitement. When we made it to the moderate thrill, it was even more basic than I had imagined from the map. But it had its purpose. I was going to make him feel the way that the g-forces and I had fallen in love years ago. We got in line and waited, up through the wooden cabin, watching the mine-shaft buggy spin in circles all around the track. I could tell Lupe was getting nervous because he began to tell every story under the sun in an attempt to take his mind off what he had already committed to. A small group of our students had also made their way to the line by now and were beginning to cheer him on across the platform. We laughed as his breathing increased as the line inched closer and closer.

Finally, it was our turn. We all loaded in, pulled down on our harnesses, and were ready to take off. Only, my harness wouldn't lock. After two or three tries, the attendant asked me to stretch my leg uncomfortably across the cabin and to bend my other leg back. He pushed down again, now grinding the metal into my pudgy thighs. He pushed and pushed, until he finally abandoned all hope. The eyes of my students widened as I was escorted off the ride. They couldn't guarantee the safety of the "larger" passengers. One of my students motioned a heart with her hands, and I tried to hold back my tears.

Just like that, I was *the fat girl who couldn't fit in the coaster*. I didn't know how I had gotten there. Maybe it was the two high-risk pregnancies, or the depression after losing a child. Maybe it was the stress-eating from working in a food desert, or the three-hour round-trip commute. Was it just laziness? After my knee injury, I hadn't been as vigilant with the gym. Or maybe it was the autoimmune disease and my inability to keep my body out of starvation mode. None of the reasons mattered now. Brick heavy, I stood on the platform watching Lupe and the other teachers twirl around, screaming in joy, and laughing in a way that I was no longer allowed. I just knew I would become my students' next meme. *See, she was the one who was so big the ride couldn't even hold her.* How did I let myself get so out of control?

I tried to gather my composure for the group. We all decided to go our separate ways. Despite the encouragement of another one of my closest friends, I was a wreck inside. I resolved that this trip would just be a literal walk in the park, a reason to add steps to my pedometer. We passed a funnel-cake stand, but I had lost my appetite. He tried to get me to try another ride, justifying that "that one was made for kids" and "you just carry your weight in your hips." He finally talked me into trying one more ride. Outside, conveniently, there was a sample seat for us "larger guests" to try before getting in line, to save us the embarrassment of the walk of shame. I snuck into the corner and got in. It latched. My friend, the ever-faithful cheerleader, took that as proof of his earlier hypothesis.

We jumped in line, though I prepared myself for the disappointment. We made our way up to the ride. I sucked everything in until my body turned blue, sliding my wide hips into the black metal harness. We were launched into the air, and my confidence in my ability to shape-shift renewed. When we descended, the knots in my chest begged for air.

But I had done it. We ran down to see the picture taken mid-flight, and I could hardly recognize myself. For a moment, I had become something else. We talked and rode a few more rides before meeting back up with the group. Someone suggested we head to the new Wonder Woman ride. I had done it once; I knew I could do it again.

Upon approaching the large marble-esque statue of the lassoed warrior, I noticed a small sample seat tucked off to the side again. It is funny what you don't notice when you don't need it. I slid my body into the trial seat. My new limits gave me a power beyond testing. Besides, even if it was a tight fit, I would fit nonetheless. We would brave my idol's beast.

We made our way between the winding lines and fiery pillars that welcomed the heroine herself. With only a few groups in front of us, the ride completely shut down, leaving some of our students suspended on the initial incline. I should've taken that as an omen. I should've gotten out of line. But only Pride knows what happens before falling. After fifteen minutes, the ride resumed. Everyone was intact and safe, but a little shaken up. Our turn finally came, and I piled into the fourth seat. The harness came down. The attendant pushed down with all his body weight, waiting for the click. I took a giant azure breath. Nothing. My heart started to feel an unfamiliar flutter. I breathed in again. Still no click. That is when I caught the goddess's eye. She looked at me like she could see past every one of my defenses. Like she knew there was a heart on the inside that wanted so badly to be my own. I tried to shake it off, but she locked in. My chest seized and I exhaled. Then my thighs started to quake. My heart pulsed heat around every extremity. My body announced itself in swell. The plastic seat exploded from my hips, and I looked down as the track in front of me bent and the line began to scatter. A voice. One I hadn't heard before, crawled up my throat and began to roar as if shaking off everything at once.

Look how I am still breathing. The failed attempts with Death. Look how I have shape-shifted with the moon. You use me, use me up, but I am a generator of my own light. A house welcoming myself home.

My body was uncontrolled, usurping all the space, and the sky welcomed it. The entire park stared up at me in wonder. I was beaming now. Radiating so brightly that no one knew what to do with me. They ran in fear. Said their hearts were too small for me. My voice crumpled the coaster and sent everything hurling toward earth. All but the statue of the brazen woman surrounded by her bowls of fire. Glancing up at me, my skin now a magnificent gold, as brilliant as I have always been.

What are we Chameleons but the greatest imposters? Convincing ourselves that we can fit into the world. That our Joy doesn't alter the body's limits. What storytellers. But there is no longer a reason to hide when so much shelter can abound.

Now when I choose to turn this house of bones into a temple for my worthy lover, I am not ashamed. I no longer hold myself in or dim myself in the shadows. Instead, I ask that he remove his shoes. His clothes. That he washes his hands and face. This here be holy ground.

I reassure him that sin hasn't found its way here for centuries. Ask that he leave every burden he has carried at the door. That he be light. Be an empty vessel. And I will teach him all the ways his body knows how to fill.

We will make ourselves a kind of sacrament. The kind that humbles him to his knees at my altar. That asks him to break my flesh and drink my wine. That makes him remember me in every iteration and sheen. That makes him kiss the stigmata of my past attempts at surviving and reminds me that I am ever resurrecting.

Then I become the kind of tabernacle that makes the songs of angels resound from the rafters at his entrance. Blessed be the slick and bending walls that push us closer together. That join our sweat in a sea of salvation. Blessed be this speaking of tongues. This trembling skin. This steeple that stretches the sanctuary. Still, the shrill of praise that permeates like Pentecost. The unveiled and open. Blessed be the fire that they shut up in my bones and the ways I let it out. Be the way I bend and be(come) one thing or another. And he and my hips are an inseparable worship. And I do not repent for pressing him down or all that runs over and out of me. And he takes every warm blessing that swells all around him. Counts it all joy. And I do not become a split-level chapel for him. Do not break or try to hold myself in. Or force myself to convert to someone else's shadowed belief. I get to be in full apotheosis. And I am not ashamed.

Our bodies, in the shape and hue they have always been, need to be seen here too. All the ways we have learned to change, praised too. For what blood holds itself in? What Joy refuses to let itself out? What legacy keeps quiet the secret to ascending? So, on the morning my daughter looks down at her legs only to screech at the missing thigh gap, I decide we get to be goddesses too. I retrieve my sheath of lies and wrap her in the armor of a story. One she can wield like her mother's name.

Why Our Knees Kiss

They say it's rickets, bone malformation, some genetic accident. They don't know the real reason some of our knees kiss and our thighs rub close. It isn't a defect. Those rumors came out of envy.

Way back, when the ground was fertile and the sugarcane was sweet, the Speight women, those on my mother's side, thrived. They descended from the Baartmans and were the wisest and most beautiful in all the South. They were the first adapters. The way a child masters a familiar song by ear is the same way the Speights took to languages. They held a library on their tongues. The most notorious thinker of them all was Lula.

Lula was a griot. That meant she carried the history of thousands of years in the grooves of her teeth. While out harvesting crops she would whisper stories to the other workers of how the sun and moon loved so hard that they began to share each other's light. Back on the plantation, the children would gather to listen to the symphony of stories strummed from her mouth. Though it wasn't always safe. The same way the Speights came together to devour their food, other hungry beasts waited for an opening to devour too.

Alligators lived on the edge of the plantation. They gained an appetite for bait babies and couldn't shake the craving. They would hide in the high grass and wait for the children to wander too far from their parents. Then they would wrestle them under and swallow them whole. But the Speight women were smarter than the gators. They grew their hips and butts round, as the perfect way to keep the children high. They would allow the children to scale their bottoms and hold on to their backs. This way, when the meadow grass got unyielding, they could see the gators coming and avoid being eaten.

This angered the gators. They much preferred the taste of melanin over turtles or deer. They plotted and schemed a way to lure the children back to the swampy ground. Lula worried for the children's safety; she had grown fond of every fire-lit cherub face who filled themselves with story. She knew they would pass them on, make stories of their own. So one day, while Lula was hunting, she overheard the gators coming up with a plan. They were going to strike in the evening: when Lula sat all the children down to listen to the last story of the night, they would creep into the village. They would strike at the story's most interesting part. When all the children were leaning in, completely entranced by Lula, they would let their guards down. Then the gators would feast. The gators thought this was a solid plan, though they didn't count on Lula's wit.

Lula gathered the women and told them what she had heard out in the highest grass. They knew the gators had to be stopped and began brainstorming a plan of their own. One woman suggested singing all the gators to sleep in Nama, since the clicks served as their own luring drumbeat. Another said to build a wall too high for the gators to climb, but then remembered the dangers of walls. Lula combed the archives of her mouth and said she had a crazy idea.

Back when the waters stood still, the Speight women watched as the ocean became stagnant. They spoke to the moon and told her that the land would perish if the water didn't begin to move. So in an effort to help, the Speight women lent their bodies to the sea's aid. They stood on the coastline and rocked their hips like an ebb and flow. The water hesitated. Then they realized that if they pressed their knees together, the friction of their thighs set off its own trance. Before they knew it, the waves were rising and falling to the motion of their hips. This hypnotism was the perfect way to stop the gators.

The women all agreed that if their hips could protect their children and teach the waves how to come and go, they must be powerful enough to confuse the gators. Lula brought each woman a piece of twine to tie around her knees. Then they lined the perimeter as the sun began to set. Lula gathered the children like always and began to tell them a story. The gators approached. They made it past the first line of shanties, but as they broke into the center, the rhythmic sway took over. The women completely shielded the children. Their magnetic orbit, lulling and powerful. The gators, on sight, began to rock without even realizing it. Before long, they were dizzy and confused and forgot why they were there in the first place. The nausea set in next, sending every gator scurrying back into the water.

The women rejoiced. And every time the persistent gators would try to get too close, the women would tie their knees and move like the waves. After a while, they no longer needed the rope. As most things adapt, so did the women. Their round hips and large bottoms swayed over kissing knees to keep all of them safe and sound. But there was always another threat lurking. Some came through the colonies' hills. Some sailed through the sea, convinced to capture the power of the trance.

But you, my dear, still hold it. In the space where your

knees kiss and your thighs spark fire. The way to tame this world. And nothing about your body, about your joy, is an accident.

We must remind ourselves who we are. For a god will soon forget their power without a believer to remind them what they have survived. And a believer must have something to praise, lest they hold too tight to false doctrine.

I have always thought I was meant to be more. As a young girl, I equated it with mansions. Teeth covered in carats of kimberlite. Long limos that stretched for years. The kinds with the fun-house reflections of a slim, happy thing.

Then my body learned what it meant to be so ravaged that it sought to hunt itself. What kind of witchcraft says that I have become a washboard. One worn down to music. My bones clanking in the bag of my flesh. Is this pleasing to the gods' ears? Is this what you seek to call sacred?

I, so small a strong wind could turn me airborne. I, spread so thin, burdened with all the feelings at once. No silence to stop them. Holding space for ten thousand souls in raw need. In charge of every decision. Tasked with everyone's fate. I become Death in that moment. One with all the power to choose if I will pass on or stay right here.

I want to choose to take off the cloak. To forget every face I have made before. So I can remember the one I own right now. What a notion, to think that we can let go and not fall. That the hands raised to me would be enough for me to stand on. For once, I would be saved. Heralded, even, for being only who I promised to be. Me and myself alone. All Black, all woman, and loved.

So here is the ask, in the way every god asks permission for a part of your heart. I am not asking that you meet Death today. But could you believe? Such a simple task you have mastered a thousand other ways. Can you stand flat-footed on the ground and love us blindly? The way faith intercedes every time you open your lungs. Trusting that the air hasn't turned to poison. Just inhaling. Belief coming in you like a poem.

Are you ready now? Repeat after me.

Today, I refuse to just mourn
the swallowed vermillion
the missing bodies in a land

full of corpse and cause,
who just want to find
their children in their own breathing beds,

Love knowing their names
like the smell of rain on a back porch
in the fresh of May.

I want to exchange their eulogies for
everlasting life.
To trade their invisible tongues

for names we speak
in prayer.
I want them to be my hymn.

Vessels big enough to engorge,
Testaments that there is still a holy somewhere.
Today, I make them an acre of good soil

Lush and Sumptuous
Flawed and worship-worthy.
I cast them in

Give them a palace in my own ears
Exalt them on a throne of trust
On the days their bodies are forced

to kaleidoscope,
Too broken to fight
for air or catch light, I will

Say Hallelujah
Say Asé
Say Bless the Lord!

Wear sackcloth and ashes
for their brimstone and flame
like they have not been lost

or capsized in excuse
or drowned in their own silence.
Praise be an unmuted tongue

Be a body shed for me
to eat, Be a light of mine
I refuse to deny anymore.

And the church says Amen.

May the Lord put a story
between me and thee
while we are absent
One from Another.

Afterword

I sat on the concrete porch of the Poetry Foundation under the sprawling poet-trees, legs crossed, in conversation with other Poetry Incubator fellows, trading home stories and struggles. It was lunch, and after a morning of working inside on community building, our skin was thirsty for the sun. A white butterfly fluttered passionately around the circle before kissing Jarvis Subia's brown skin. He smiled familiarly. Then he told us that in Mexican mythology, butterflies symbolize the ancestors—that they visit often. My Black skin grew green with envy. It is not that I sought to be anything more than what I was. I only wanted to know exactly what *that* was.

I began to recount my early years as a young reader. One of my favorite memories was when my mother brought home a larger-than-lap Anansi storybook that was narrated by Denzel Washington. I sat in front of the cassette player with my oversize foam headphones, playing and replaying the tape, as my fingers danced over each word. From the very first drumbeat, there was something about that book that felt like a distant homeland coming into the light. I played it until the tape sagged out of the plastic casing; I wound it back up with a pencil and played it some more. Every time I listened, the story lifted off the page and became more real, in much the same way the Bible did for me on Sunday mornings. Both texts gave me context and instruction on how to navigate this world both Black and human. But for all their vast and beautiful impact, one or two books could not satisfy my ferocious appetite to understand the world around me. This moment with Jarvis only further aggravated that gnawing itch that I had suppressed by some method of adulthood. From there, I began to dig even deeper.

I revisited W. E. B. Du Bois's ideas on "double consciousness," in which he explains we must understand the duality of ourselves as "American" and "Negro." While Paul Bunyan offers us an American tale and Anansi offers us a Black narrative, they lack something in their ability to merge both thoughts into a singular origin. The classical literary canon offers no remedies for this. Its limited inclusion of Black voices—except the few that sneak into a *Norton's Anthology* every year—asks us to accept the tales of Greeks and Romans, Zeus and Jesus, as the most popular and superior mythologies of how the world began. Black Americans have few choices between creationism and Greek mythology to define the world for ourselves; a world that moves and births an entirely different experience from that of Abraham or Icarus.

I have spent years trying to research beyond the abysmal wall of slavery to locate roots that tie my family to one of hundreds of African cultures, and I am not alone in this. The proliferation of Black subscribers to sites like Ancestry .com and MyHeritage.com speaks to this longing we share. However, these efforts often leave us devoid of any real answers, clinging to African traditions and stories we have no quantifiable connection to, outside of our abundance of melanin. Simultaneously, Black American culture has had limited room for mythmaking. While Octavia Butler and Zora Neale Hurston, among others, breathed life into the early pillars, the creation of myths has remained elusive.

Mythmaking in and of itself is the art of creating a history that you choose to believe is true. When have Black people in the Americas had the time to create a history outside the one they were just trying to survive? And in the few moments we get to dream aloud, who is there to record our origins beyond a whitewashed dictation?

The Black American timeline isn't the same as those painted in the hieroglyphics or marked in the Dick and Jane grammar series my mother used to teach me to read. We arrived much later and more viciously, under someone else's guise. Virginia Hamilton's *The People Could Fly* tells us of our superpower to transcend slavery and return to Africa through flight. This elegy to captives willing to drown themselves rather than be slaves has served us well for decades. But what do we do with the stories of those who chose to stay after the Great Flight? This rebirth isn't quite explained in the stories of Brer Bear and Brer Rabbit. Rather, it shifts our focus to capturing the truth of what our history books try to erase. What happens when the children of those characters in Hamilton's stories begin to ask questions?

Another moment of reflection was sparked when Houston's 2019 Youth Poet Laureate, Jackson Neal, asked me to join their podcast called *Myth City*. The interviews captured local myths of the residents of Houston. They asked me to consider what cultural myths I grew up believing prior to the recording. I spent two weeks spiraling. I went back to Anansi, but there was something missing. It was more borrowed than mine. Then I thought of my mother telling my brother and me that she had eyes in the back of her head. She used this to scare us out of making poor decisions when she wasn't around. I truly believed that my mother could see through walls. She always seemed to know what we were doing, and for a long time I bought into that mysticism. I rambled something to that effect on the podcast, but my ideas were sparse and disconnected. I was still figuring it out. When I returned home, I decided to write the myth of how my mother's kind received the eyes. The first story in this collection was my initial explanation, and it opened up a world of possibilities.

However, my memories alone didn't give me enough to carry me through this act of creating my own personal mythology, or biomythography, as it's referred to in Audre Lorde's *Zami: A New Spelling of My Name*. In fact, the more research I did, the more I came to realize that this mythmoir idea of mine wasn't a new thought per se. For generations, writers like Maxine Hong Kingston had been experimenting with the crosshatch of cultural stories and lived experiences. However, I found few Black writers who were bridging into creating their own mythology, as most depended on established myths from the African diaspora to make the connections for them. To my mind, this was half the length of the journey.

As I embarked upon creating the other half, I found myself consumed by the myths of various countries. I dove deeper into cultures outside my own as a means of creating a framework I could build these new stories by. In the way that Jarvis's traditions opened my world to further consider our relationship with nature, these other cultural tales gave me new lenses through which to consider my memories. My need for more drove me to find the *Myths, Folklore, and Fairytales* podcast on Spotify. It was engaging and interesting. Also, it provided me the convenience of listening to it on my commute to and from work. The oral tradition and language barriers that would have been my downfall if I had tried to find and read many of these tales were removed. I started to deconstruct those stories and connect them to my own experiences.

One of the first myths to intrigue me was the myth of Momotaro in Japanese folklore. Translated "Peach Boy," he is a fierce fighter who was born from a peach that his parents found floating down a river. I began to connect with the idea of using southern agriculture as a vehicle to physically birth new ideas. The peach as a symbol of Georgia grounded me in my southern heritage. It reminded me of the motherland of Black America: the South. I began to consider that setting every story there might be the most honest way to start. While we have stories that stretch far beyond that, including my family tales that live primarily in California and Michigan, most of us have ties back to the Deep South in some way. I started to think about what types of fruits and vegetables would birth my family in the most fantastical telling of my history. This is what led me to the gourd baby story.

From there, I started to reimagine language in a different way. Now the phrases of my mother and grandmother began to seem less colloquial and more tied to stories that had been lost along the way. One of my mother's favorite sayings is "If the Lord say the same and the creek don't rise." Growing up in California, there were few creeks to justify this. But the South and her roots in Tuscaloosa, Alabama, cried different tales. I began to think about a world where the creek rose or the Lord didn't say the same. This story was never fully imagined, but this ability to tap into our tongues shifted the way I began to consider my own heritage. I started writing down every story that my mother told me about the women that came before me, hoping to find some new entry point into the creative process of developing mythology.

My need to create became an incessant and necessary means to explain things to myself and my children. When my daughter asked me why she had no thigh gap or when I visited a plantation, the southern haven of oppression, for the first time, I needed new paths. But this was not just a need that lived under my roof. My friends started to share their stories with me. Social media posts that discussed mothers' sayings started trending on my timeline. I began to realize that there need to be stories that work to bridge the cultural gap that slavery severed from our tongues and hid under the ships' decks. This work was the continued effort to erect a house of culture on the foundations of the stories captured by Henry Louis Gates Jr. in his anthology of African American folktales. This work leads in self-reliance. We held the power, much like the creators of Kwanzaa, to reshape what Black American culture believes, at its core, about itself. We were not beyond the moment of seeking truth.

Mythmaking isn't a lie. It is our moment to take the privilege of our own creativity in Black Mythology and use it to fill in the gaps in literature that colonization has tried to steal from us. It is us choosing to write the tales that our children pull strength from. It is hijacking history for the ignorance in its closets. This, a truth that must start with the women.

During Bible study one day with my eight-year-old daughter, I introduced her to the godhead: the Father, the Son, and the Holy Spirit. To which she replied, "Mom, where is the mother and the daughter?" This sentiment was as

AFTERWORD

sweet as it was telling. Are we not made in the image of God too? While Ruth and Esther took their places among the few women who emerged in the Bible, they never ascended to the level of significance of men like King David. The number of women who identified as Moorish or Black drew an even less impressive number. I began to look elsewhere, examining the oral and recorded mythology of Black American women. This only provided a more disturbing trend. Those in these stories were always depicted as witch or sorcerer. This, coupled with the stereotypical views of the mammy, the Jezebel, and the militant only further angered me.

I have struggled against these assumptions my whole life. At home, my mother tried to undercut them with images of Cleopatra and Nefertiti. I honestly felt very little connection to either of them culturally. I wanted a woman on this side of the Atlantic to reveal what I already knew: that the multifaceted Black woman is none and all of these simultaneously. She is not one who can be limited by a caricature. She is mighty in her own right. Even then, I craved a mythology I could not find.

We often say that Black women are magic; maybe a better sentiment is that Black women are mythological. We are supernatural phenomena. We explain nature and the divine. To survive, we birthed a planet full of contradictions. We can write our future and rewrite our past while fluttering in the middle.

Acknowledgments

To God be the glory for the bravery, wisdom, and permission to create this work. Only God could wake me up at three a.m. with fully formed stories that even I didn't always understand. I am humbled to be a vessel.

To my mother, Patricia, the woman who taught me how to be a woman. I will be forever indebted to you for your example, your love, your strength, and your willingness to let me write honestly and without consequence. You have always been my biggest cheerleader. May the world see you as brilliantly and love you as fiercely as I do. To my late father, Carl, thank you for teaching me that I have always been worthy of love and that every odd thing about me wasn't a mistake. I know you are screaming from Heaven, "That's my baby!" I love you both.

To Grandma Bettye, Grandma Geneva, Aunt Zora,

Great-Grandma Ida Mae, and every other woman I have known deeply in my bones and DNA, you have shown me that there is no limit to a Black woman's resilience and strength. I love you dearly.

To my husband, Josh, you may be the best decision I ever made. Thank you for completing me, for challenging me, and for believing in me when I wasn't sure. To my little loves, Olivet and Julius, thank you for all the times you let me sneak away to my office and write when all you wanted was time with your mother. This is because of y'all. I love you cow-million, yesterday and still!

To my brother and sisters, thank you for the memories that made this book and my life so colorful.

To Kirby Kim, my amazing agent, you constantly challenge me and make me a more intentional writer. Thank you for fighting for this work and helping me give it a home that knew exactly what it needed. To my editor, Retha Powers, how did I get so lucky to create this book with you? You have a knack for bringing out the best in people and in work. I am so grateful for you and your heart and piercing insight.

To Bloomsday Literary, Kate, Jess, and Phuc, you have had my back since *Newsworthy*. Thank you for seeing me. For loving me. For reading everything. And for saying I was on the right track. (And the occasional Tiff's treats to get me there.)

To my tribe: Marcell Murphy, Emanuelee Bean, Jeremyah Payne, Jordan Simpson, Desmond Jones, Erica Cuscina,

Monica and Michael Adeeko, Meggie Monihan, Malaysia English, Tabitha Conaway, Sam and Marquis Smith, Dulcie Veluthakaran, Lupe and Jasminne Mendez, Pierre and Flo Smith, Yolan and Ashley Young, Joe Palmore, Brandon Harrison, and my American Lyric Theater family, I love each and every one of you for standing by me on this long journey. Thank you for listening to me talk about this book for three years, in and out of context. You really are the best village a girl could have. A special thanks to my girls Kate Williams, Vogue Robinson, Monica Davidson, Jasmine Barnes, Robin Davidson, Rayla Crawford, and Emilie Koenig. Thank you for answering the late-night calls, for having the hard conversations, for comforting me, and for reminding me that sisterhood defies space, time, and color.

Jackson Neal, you beautiful human. I know you thought I was helping you with your podcast, but you were helping loose something in me. Thank you for being the student I could learn so much from. You will never know how our time at Metafour and beyond has made me a better writer and person. To my students at HSPVA, especially Mariah Adeeko and Aanisah Johnson, thank you for reading the first drafts of your crazy teacher, for reminding me to keep writing because there are people waiting for these stories. To Houston Grand Opera, *Fjords*, the *Texas Observer*, thank you for bringing portions of this work to light in all the magnificent ways that you have.

For every reader that picks up this book, thank you for

taking time and energy to read this. May you realize that God made no mistakes in shaping you. May you find a way to praise all that you've suffered through as much as you praise the grace that pulled you from it. May you feel more seen, more accepted, and more at home in your own skin. And the church says . . .

About the Author

Deborah D.E.E.P Mouton is an internationally known writer, director, performer, and critic and the first Black poet laureate of Houston, Texas. She is the author of the 2019 poetry collection *Newsworthy*, which was a finalist for the Writers' League of Texas Book Award and received honorable mention for the Summerlee Book Prize. Her poems have garnered her a Pushcart nomination and have been translated into multiple languages. She has been a contributing writer for *Glamour*, *Texas Monthly*, *Muzzle*, and ESPN's *Andscape*. Her work ranges from writing stage plays and librettos for operas such as *Marian's Song* and the choreo-poem *Plumshuga* to storytelling through film. She currently resides in Houston, Texas.